This book belongs to

SARAH

Children's Stories From

THE
BIBLE

For Michael, Michelle and Melanie - S.P.
For Katie and Sydney - A.Y.G.
For Peggy O'Connor and Michael O'Connor and Brother Thomas - I.A.

This edition published in 2009 by Key Porter Books
Six Adelaide Street East, Tenth Floor
Toronto, Ontario, Canada M5C 1H6
www.keyporter.com

Devised and produced by The Templar Company plc,
The Granary, North Street, Dorking, Surrey, RH4 1DN, UK

09 10 11 10 9 8 7 6 5 4 3 2 1

Library and Archives Canada Cataloguing in Publication
Children's stories from the Bible / editor: Templar Publishing ;
illustrators: Anne Yvonne Gilbert and Ian Andrew.
ISBN 978-1-55470-153-7
1. Bible stories, English. I. Andrew, Ian P., 1962- II. Gilbert,
Anne Yvonne
BS551.2.C485 2009   220.9'505   C2008-905009-6

Nihil Obstat

The Scripture quotations contained herein are from
The New Revised Standard Version of the Bible,
Anglicized Edition, copyright © 1989, 1995 by the
Division of Christian Education of the National Council
of the Churches of Christ in the United States of America,
and are used by permission. All rights reserved.

ISBN 13: 978-1-55470-153-7
ISBN 10: 1-55470-153-8

Consultant SU BOX
Designer JANIE LOUISE HUNT
Editor LIBBY HAMILTON
Maps AMANDA HALL

Printed in China

Children's Stories From
THE
BIBLE

Stories retold by *Saviour Pirotta*
Colour art by *Anne Yvonne Gilbert*
Monochrome art by *Ian Andrew*

KEY PORTER BOOKS

The Old Testament

The New Testament

Introduction

As a small child I lived in a community whose social calendar was arranged around Christian festivals. Our island also had a strong oral story-telling tradition — every festival, every celebration, came with a wealth of stories that made the Bible and the gospels come alive.

Those stories of my childhood made me want to become a writer. I spent days collecting all the stories I could find, retelling them to friends or turning them into little plays. By the time I left school, there were other influences in my life, but as my career blossomed, I still kept an interest in Bible stories, so it was a great pleasure to be asked to write this collection.
It had been some time since I had read the Bible closely — would the stories have the same resonance, inspire the same awe that they did when I was a small child?

This project was a huge undertaking. Each retelling presented a different challenge — some stories were very familiar, while others were little known; one might be too long or detailed for a young reader, while another needed extra colour to bring the events to life. As I worked, I was drawn back to those days in my own childhood when just a few words from the storyteller would make the Bible come alive for me.

I humbly hope that I have carried on this tradition and that my retellings in this book will make some of the most important, the most influential stories in the world come alive for you too.

SAVIOUR PIROTTA

In the beginning

when God created the heavens and the earth,

the earth was a formless void and darkness

covered the face of the deep, while a wind from

God swept over the face of the waters.

Then God said, "Let there be light";

and there was light. And God saw

that the light was good.

GENESIS 1:1-5

The Old Testament

The Creation

Then God said, "Let the earth bring forth living creatures of every kind: cattle and creeping things and wild animals."

GENESIS 1:1-2

In the beginning, before God had made anything, there was nothing. There was no air, no sound, no time, no light. There was no solid or liquid, just God, who had always been there, moving alone in the darkness.

Then God created the heavens and the earth. But the earth was empty and barren, a scary place. Deep waters covered its surface, churning and swirling endlessly.

So God said, *"Let there be light."*

And there was light, faint and red at first, then white and dazzling. Then it became soft again, pink and pleasant to look at. God marvelled at how lovely the light was. He called it day. When it faded, he called the darkness night.

That was the first day of the world.

On the second day, when the light appeared again, God made the sky. Bright blue, it covered the earth from one end to the other, like a vast dome.

That was the second day of the world.

On the third day, God gathered the water into huge pools he called seas. They sparkled in the sunlight, a bright blue to match the sky above them. Land appeared where the water had been, muddy and brown. It was flat in places, nearly touching the sky in others. God had made plains and mountains. He made valleys too, and caves, reaching deep into the bowels of the newborn earth.

But the world looked barren with just rocks, stones and mud, so God said, *"Let the earth be covered in greenery."* Grass sprouted out of the earth, turning it a

vivid green.
Creepers snaked over
the bare rocks. Plants
grew out of the drying mud,
with leaves of every shape and size.
Plants with huge vegetables and flowers
of every colour that perfumed the air.
  Trees rose out of the ground, their
branches reaching towards the sky, their
roots anchored deep within the earth.
Many were covered in fruit – apples,
mangos, pears and figs, delicious things
  to eat, although there was nobody
        yet to eat them.
        That was the third day of the
        world.
        On the fourth day, God
        made the sun and the moon.
        The sun he created so it
        would shed light on the
        earth during the day. The
        moon he made for the night,
        to fill the world with its silvery

beauty.
He created
stars too, millions
upon millions
of them, and
he scattered
them across the
velvety night sky,
where they hung
in twinkling
garlands. That
was the fourth
day of the
world.

On the fifth day, God said, "*Let the waters be filled with living creatures.*" Countless sea creatures appeared.

There were sharks and swordfish, dolphins, and giant octopuses with huge tentacles. Strange-looking creatures that stayed at the bottom of the sea, some with lights on their heads to show the way. Fish that preferred the warmer waters of the surface, darting and diving, some even flying out of the waves with their fins. God made whales; gentle, hulking creatures that spouted water out of their heads. He created jellyfish, crabs and little shells that glittered like diamonds along the shore.

Then God said, "*Let there be creatures in the air, too.*"

There was a rustling of feathers, a beating of wings and birds appeared in the sky, chirping, squawking and calling. They took to the sky, they settled on the trees, they drank from the waters and nibbled at the fruit on the plants and trees. There were thousands of birds: big eagles and small sparrows, red robins, blue jays, green budgies, yellow canaries, white doves, purple macaws, blackbirds and grey nightingales. They sang and chirped and explored the world and skies around them.

That was the fifth day of the world.

On the sixth day God said, "*Let there be creatures on the face of the earth.*"

Out of nowhere came the animals: hippos and elephants, lions and tigers, deer, bears and thousands upon thousands of others. There were reptiles too and insects that crawled, hopped or flew on little wings like the birds. Some animals preferred the lush jungles and thick forests. Gentle creatures, like cows, sheep and cats, liked the open spaces. Then God scooped up some wet earth and with it made two new creatures that looked like him, mirroring his image. He called these creatures Man and Woman.

He breathed life into them and, as their lungs filled with air, their eyes opened. Their arms reached up to the warmth of the sun and they stood up, blinking in amazement at the new world around them.

God blessed them and said to them, *"I have made you to enjoy and look after all the things I created. You have fruit to eat and water to drink. You are in charge of the world, use it to enjoy your life. Have many children so that they may spread around the world and fill it."*

That was the sixth day of the world and God's work was finally done. He looked around him and he was pleased with everything he had created.

On the seventh day, God rested.

Adam and Eve

*God said, "You shall not eat of the fruit
of the tree that is in the middle of the garden,
nor shall you touch it, or you shall die."*

GENESIS 3:3

Now God made a beautiful garden for Adam and Eve, the first man and woman, to live in. He called it Eden and he filled it with soft grass to walk on and plants and trees bearing all kinds of delicious fruit. He put a stream in it too, so that Adam and Eve would have clear water to drink and to bathe in.

In the middle of the garden, God planted a tree, with enormous branches casting shadows on the grass. He called it the tree of knowledge.

"You may pick fruit from any other tree in the garden," he said to them. *"But I do not want you to eat the fruit from the tree of knowledge. If you do, you will die."*

For a while Adam and Eve obeyed. They helped themselves to luscious fruits from all the other trees in the garden: oranges, mangoes and ripe avocados with nut-brown skins. But they kept away from the tree of knowledge.

Then one day, Eve was picking the berries that grew in the shade of the tree. That tree. She heard a rustling among the branches and looked up to see a snake, its golden scales glinting in the sun.

"You are picking fruit," said the snake, darting out his forked tongue.

"Just these berries," said Eve.

"No other fruit?" asked the snake, curling around a branch.

"Not from this tree," said Eve hurriedly. "God told us not to eat from it. If we do, we will die."

"Did he now?" sniggered the snake. "This is the tree of knowledge. If you eat its fruit, you will not die – you'll become as wise as God himself."

The snake flicked his forked tongue and a fruit from the tree of knowledge fell to the ground. It rolled right up to

Eve's feet and stopped. She picked it up. It felt cool and heavy in her hands, like a stone from the stream. She wondered what it would taste like.

"I might have a little bite," she thought. "One little bite couldn't possibly do any harm, could it?"

"Certainly not," hissed the snake, reading her thoughts. "And think of all the things you'll learn. One little bite, tiny as a bird's, and you'll be as wise as God and just as powerful."

All that cleverness! All that wisdom and power for just one little bite of fruit was so tempting. CRUNCH!

"What are you doing?" Adam had heard the sound of teeth biting into fruit and raced across the grass.

Eve held out the fruit. "Have some, it won't kill you. The snake said it will make us as wise as God himself."

Adam hesitated, but only for a moment. If Eve had eaten some, why

couldn't he? CRUNCH! He took a bite, leaving teeth marks in the pale flesh.

Almost at once, there were was a rustle among the fruit trees. Perfumed wind nodded the branches, scattering petals. God had come to walk in the shade of the garden.

"*Adam! Eve!*" Where were his creations, his new companions who usually ran to meet him?

They were hiding among the bushes, close to the tree of knowledge, the knowledge of good and evil. He could hear their hearts beating rapidly. They were scared of him, terrified.

"Eve told me to do it," stammered Adam, standing up, shielding his eyes with his hands.

"The snake tricked me," moaned Eve.

"*Only one tree,*" said God sadly. "*I gave you all the other fruit in the Garden. You could have eaten any of it. Why couldn't you obey this one command?*"

He turned away from them in his sadness and a hot desert wind rippled through the magnificent garden, chasing away the shade, the coolness, the peace.

"You have disobeyed me and for this you must leave the Garden of Eden. From now on, you will have to work hard to gather fruit and vegetables from the earth. The toil will make you grow old and feeble until you finally die. I made you from soil and when you die you will become soil once more."

stones and jagged rocks. Angels appeared at the entrance to the Garden, each one carrying a flaming sword, and the gates closed behind them, hiding the beautiful garden, the trees, the streams and the tame animals forever.

Adam and Eve shivered. It was cold out here, freezing. The ground was hard under their feet and there were

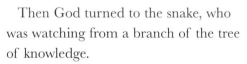

Then God turned to the snake, who was watching from a branch of the tree of knowledge.

"You vile, wicked creature. Everyone shall know that you are the lowest of the low. From this day forward, you shall be man's enemy. You shall crawl on your belly through the dirt and the mud."

The snake hissed with pain and fell to the ground. Adam and Eve saw him crawling through the grass, his belly leaving a trail behind him. Then they looked up and were no longer in the Garden of Eden but outside it, in a terrible wilderness strewn with huge

no fruit trees anywhere in sight, just stunted bushes. A chill wind blew. "What are we going to eat?" wondered Eve.

Adam pulled some weeds from the ground. They tasted bitter in his mouth and he spat them out again.

Somewhere beyond the jagged rocks a wild animal howled. It too was hungry. Eve pointed to a cave and they ran into it for shelter. The sun set, leaving behind it a dark, moonless night.

Adam and Eve huddled together in their cave. It was their first night outside the garden and they were miserable, terrified and hungry.

If only they had not disobeyed God.

My Brother's Keeper

The Lord said to Cain... "If you do well,
will you not be accepted? And if you do not do well,
sin is lurking at the door; its desire is for you."

GENESIS 4:6–7

Adam and Eve had two sons: Cain and Abel. Cain loved growing things: vegetables, grain and even fruit, which he would give to his mother. Abel preferred to look after his father's flock. He would take them out on the hills, where the grass grew thick and small streams trickled down.

Adam and Eve were very proud of their children.

"Do not disobey the Lord like we did," they would say when the family huddled around the fire at night. "Learn from our mistakes."

When summer came, Abel's sheep had many lambs; the countryside was filled with their bleating. Cain did well too. His fields were full of crops, growing in neat rows across the land.

"You must offer a sacrifice to God," said Adam to his sons. "It's our way of showing him that we are thankful for the harvest. And it will show God that we trust him and are willing to obey his commands. So make sure you offer some of the best harvest he gave you."

Abel rushed to get a lamb. He found the fattest one in the flock and offered it to God on a stone altar his father had built. A breeze caught the thick, billowing smoke and lifted it up into the heavens.

"God is pleased with Abel's sacrifice," said Eve to her husband as they watched from their cave.

Cain also hurried to his field. What could he offer God? Some of his fruit, his grain or his vegetables? I can't sacrifice any of the fruit or vegetables, thought Cain. We might need them for the winter. And what a waste to burn grain. Surely God would not want me to set fire to it? After all, God does not actually need my grain.

That was it then. Cain was not going to sacrifice fruit, grain or vegetables.

He chose a bale of straw. After all, what did it matter which part of the harvest was burnt on the altar? No one could see anything through the thick smoke.

Cain piled the straw on to the altar and set it alight. He was expecting it to catch fire immediately, but the wind blew out the feeble flame.

"God is not pleased with Cain's sacrifice," said Eve.

Cain tried to light the straw again, but the flame kept going out.

"God prefers Abel to me," he muttered to himself. "Everything he does is always better."

Just then he spied Abel walking past with his sheep.

"Off to the hills again?" he said. "I'll walk with you awhile." He picked up a heavy branch to use as a walking stick and caught up with his brother.

"God was more pleased with your sacrifice than mine," Cain started abruptly.

Abel said nothing.

"I'm certain mother and father were pleased with you too," he continued. "They always are."

"I'm sure they love us both the same," said Abel.

"They love you more," said Cain. Now all the disappointment he'd felt at God's rejection of his stingy sacrifice was turning into

anger – anger aimed at the person closest to him, his young brother.

"They talk about you all the time. I might as well not exist!"

"Perhaps you should tell them how you feel about things," said Abel.

"They won't take any notice," fumed Cain, thumping his stick on the ground.

Abel, feeling sorry for his brother, fumbled in his sack for some bread.

"Mother made it this morning. Have some. It will calm you down."

Now Cain was trembling with fury. Eve had never given him bread to take to the fields! It was the last straw, seeing that fresh bread in his brother's hand. Cain raised his stick and, almost before he knew it, he struck him. There was a horrific sound as the stick cracked against Abel's skull. Abel reached out with both hands. Then he keeled over on to the ground. He was dead. Cain had killed his brother.

The voice was coming from behind the clouds, high up in the sky.

"I don't know," shouted back Cain, running faster and faster. "Am I supposed to look after my brother? Haven't I got enough to do already?"

"Why did you kill your brother?" asked God. *"I rejected your offering because it was not the best you had. He had nothing to do with your shame."*

Cain lowered his head.

"That will teach you to be better than me!" shouted Cain.

He thought for a moment and then was seized by panic. If God had been angry at him for sacrificing damp straw, surely he would be furious at Cain for killing his brother?

The young man started to run. Away from home, away from his parents, away from his fields. But there was no running away from God.

"Cain, where is your brother?"

"Because you have committed murder, you will wander around the earth without finding any peace, any joy in life."

That was the last time Cain heard God's voice. He kept on running and running till he came to a strange land far from home. But no matter how much distance he put between himself and his family, he could never forget what he had done to his innocent brother. He had to live with that guilt for the rest of his life.

Two by Two

*"And of every living thing, of all flesh,
you shall bring two of every kind into the ark,
to keep them alive with you."*

GENESIS 6:19

Adam and Eve had more children besides Cain and Abel. Their descendants spread all over the world, working the land, building homes and hunting for food. But after a while these people forgot the real God. They built false gods out of stone and worshipped them instead. They fought amongst themselves, too. They lied, they cheated, they even killed one another.

"*I am sorry that I made all these living things,*" God said to himself. "*I shall wipe them all out and I shall start afresh.*"

Then he saw a family far below. The father was offering sacrifice to him. The man's wife, his sons and their wives were around him, praying.

"*I shall spare that family,*" said God, "*they are still good.*"

The man offering the sacrifice was Noah. God spoke to him while he was sleeping and said, "*Do not be afraid, I am your God. I have decided to destroy the world and all the living creatures on it. But I shall spare you and your family, and two of every kind of animal. So build yourself an ark. Make it sound and watertight, for I am going to send a great rain that will flood the earth.*"

When Noah woke up he passed on God's instructions to his sons, Ham, Shem and Japheth. They started building the ark right away. With axes, saws and knives they chopped down trees and made planks. They nailed them together, forming a huge boat, and they covered it with tar so that it was watertight. A huge crowd gathered around them, inspecting the work and passing useless comments.

"What are you building, Noah, a ship?" laughed one man.

"Going sailing, then, Noah? Aren't you too old to leave home?"

"Gone soft in the head, poor man. Him, his three boys and their wives – stark raving mad the lot of them. It comes from only worshipping one god."

"An invisible god that doesn't exist!"

Noah and his children took no notice of the crowds. They worked all day and night, day after day, night after night, stopping only to eat and drink. They prayed while they worked, carrying supplies on to the ark, stocking it for the journey ahead. When at last the ark was ready, there was a great shaking of trees in the forest nearby and the animals started arriving: big animals that trampled the dust with their mighty steps, small animals that bounded up the gangplank into the ark. Birds came too, and reptiles, and insects that did not have to use the gangplank at all but flew in through the windows. Two by two they came, until the ark was crammed full of roaring, hooting, stamping, howling, hissing creatures.

There was a flash of lightning. The great ark door slammed shut, pushed by God's invisible hands.

It started to rain. Only a little bit at first, so the rowdy crowds outside kept calling.

"Hey, Noah, you had better tell your wife to take in the washing!"

"Ham, you won't need a bath on the ark if this rain keeps up."

And the rain did keep up. Soon there were streams swirling around the crowd's feet. Then it was up to their knees, their hips. Some people started to feel scared then.

"Noah, let us in! We're friends."

The clouds in the sky got thicker and darker. The rain got heavier. Inside the ark, Noah and his family could hear it drumming on the roof, drowning all other sounds. The animals, awed by the noise, fell silent. At sunset, they could feel the water lifting the ark off the ground. The timber creaked, frightening the animals.

"Sssh, don't fret," said Noah. "God will look after us."

They were off then, carried by the strong currents. Outside, the water level rose above the trees, then the houses and the hills. For forty days and forty nights, the rains kept coming, pouring down in big sheets until even the mountains were drowned. Then they stopped, quite suddenly, and there was a great stillness over the earth; everything and everyone outside the ark had perished.

"Father, can we go out?" asked Shem.

"No son, there is no land to walk on."

The whole family waited, eking out the food they had left on board. Many days passed, with the sun shining on the water that stretched in every direction to the horizon. Then, early

one morning, they felt a bump under the ark. It had come to rest on rocky ground. Noah took a dove from its cage and thrust it out of the window. It flew around for a little while, then returned to his hands.

"There is nowhere for it to rest yet," said Noah. "The world is still covered in water. We must have landed on top of a mountain."

Seven days later, they tried again. This time the dove returned with a twig in its beak.

"It has found an olive tree!" said Noah. "We can go out soon."

They waited another week before releasing the dove again. All the family waited by the window for it to return. But the dove didn't come back, so they knew it had found dry ground.

"Go out of the ark," said God. *"And bring the animals out with you."*

They pushed open the heavy door. The wood resisted, then fell away from the entrance. Noah and his family stepped blinking into the sunshine. All around them new plants were poking through puddles and muddy earth.

When Shem, Ham and Japheth released the animals, they charged out of the ark, eager to taste fresh grass, stretch their legs and enjoy the sunshine.

Noah built an altar on the mountain top and offered a sacrifice to God.

"Thank you," he said, "for saving our lives and looking after us."

"You must have many children," said God, speaking from the smoke of the burning sacrifice. *"I want the earth to be full of people again, people who will obey me as their God. Never again shall all living creatures be wiped out. I promise never to drown the earth again."*

A flutter of wings made Noah and his children look up. An immense arch was straddling the clearing sky, shimmering with seven bright colours.

"Behold," said God, *"this is the sign that will remind you of my promise. When you see it, no matter how hard it rains, you will know that you are safe and that I will keep my word."*

Noah and his family gasped in wonder. They were looking at the first rainbow.

The Tower of Babel

"Come, let us build ourselves a city,
and a tower with its top in the heavens,
and let us make a name for ourselves."

GENESIS 11:4

Before long, Noah's children had multiplied. They spread out around the world, finding new homes, setting up farms and building towns and villages where they could live in safe communities. In those days, everyone spoke the same language, so whenever people travelled they could always make themselves understood and strangers quickly became friends.

Now one group of people settled on a great plain. It had two rivers which made the land in between rich and fertile. The ground was flat – easy to till and work for crops. The people

settled there. They built homes and streets and soon they became rich from selling their crops and the fish they caught in the two rivers. The leader of these rich people was a great hunter. He would go out every morning to hunt wild animals – fierce creatures that might attack his people.

One day, returning from a hunt with his advisors, this leader said, "I believe we are by far the most successful community in the world. We shall build a great city to show everyone how powerful we are."

"Yes, yes!" agreed his advisors.

"We can make really good bricks and strong mortar that will not crumble easily in the rain. Let us build a great tower in the centre of our city that can be seen from miles around."

Everyone nodded in agreement.

"We'll build the tower so high, it will touch the sky."

So the men set to work, baking bricks and mixing mortar. The women joined in the work songs and brought food to keep up the men's strength. Soon they had built a great city surrounded by a strong wall to keep out the enemy. With tree-lined streets, bathing pools and perfumed gardens, it was magnificent – the most beautiful place in the world.

Then they started building the tower – the one they wanted everyone to see from across the plains and the deserts. Brick by brick they built it, using mortar so strong, the rain could not crumble it. Soon the tower reached up to the sky, poking through the clouds.

God saw the tower from the heavens and he was not pleased.

"*Human beings are getting ideas above their station,*" he said to himself. "*If I let them finish this tower, they will believe they are as great and powerful as I am. No, I must remind them that they should be humble.*"

God passed his hand over the tower and, for a moment, there was a return to night – a total eclipse of the sun. The workmen paused to blink.

"What was that?"

"What happened?"

"What did you say?"

"Could you repeat that?"

It was chaos – no one knew what anyone else was saying.

Suddenly, all the men and women seemed to be talking in different languages. There was confusion. Why couldn't they all understand each other like they had before? Men started arguing, waving their hands at each other in a bid to continue their work.

"Hand me that brick."

"Pass me that rope."

It was no use.

No one understood a word his neighbour said. They had all suddenly become strangers, suspicious of each other. Work on the tower ground to a halt. People became frightened. Their leader tried to speak to them, but no one could understand what he was trying to say.

"We must leave this place," they said to their families who, thankfully, still spoke the same language as them. "We're better off on our own, where we can all understand each other. You can't get on with people who behave like strangers."

So whole families started leaving the great plain right away, scattering across different countries. They were eager to set up their own communities, where eclipses didn't suddenly change the way your neighbour spoke. The tower stood abandoned only half way up to the star-filled sky. Soon it fell into ruins. The strong mortar turned dry and crumbled; the bricks fell to the ground. No one could see it from across the plains anymore.

The city in which the tower had stood soon became a legend, the stuff of campfire stories. It was nicknamed Babel, perhaps because, on the last day of its glory, everyone seemed to just be stumbling around saying "Ba, ba, ba," to their old friends.

Abraham and Sarah

*He brought him outside and said, "Look towards
heaven and count the stars, if you are able to count them."
Then he said to him, "So shall your descendants be."*

GENESIS 15:5

From the great city of Ur, where kings sat on golden thrones, there came a rich man called Abraham and his wife, Sarah. Settling in Haran, they had everything they wanted: food, warm clothes, great herds of cattle and flocks of sheep, even money and silver. Only one thing was missing in their life: a son – an heir to inherit Abraham's wealth.

One night, while Abraham was dozing by the fire, he heard a strange voice.

"Abraham, I am your God. Trust me and you will be father to a great nation."

Abraham wanted to say, "How can I be the father of a great nation? I have no children and my wife and I are getting old." But his faith in God was strong, so he said nothing, believing that God could make anything happen.

"Set out to a new land," said God, *"There I will keep my promise to you."*

Abraham's family had been nomads before settling in Haran, so he had all he needed for the long journey: tents, camels, great baskets to carry food and sheepskins for water. When everything was packed, Abraham set out with his family, slaves and servants in tow.

"Where are we going, master?"

"Why are we leaving this city? You are loved and respected – you have so many friends here."

But Abraham took no heed of his servants. He and Sarah led the way out of the city, into the hot desert. They walked until their feet were covered in blisters and the hot sun had burnt their skin. At long last they came to a country called Canaan, where the grass was green, the vistas were open and the streams were sweet to drink. They pitched their tents in the shade of some trees, at a place known as Mamre.

There, Abraham again heard the voice of God.

"*This is the country I will give to your descendants. Abraham, look up at the sky. Do you see how many stars there are? I will give you as many descendants as there are stars in the heaven.*"

Every night after that, Abraham would sit outside his tent and look up at the vast skies, marvelling at how many stars there were. Would he really have that many descendants? He and Sarah were growing old. Their skin was wrinkling, their bones becoming brittle. When would they have a son to carry on their family?

Then one day three men were seen walking up the hill towards Abraham's tents. Visitors. The slaves and the servants burst into activity. They laid fresh rugs in their master's tent. They filled bowls with perfumed water. They put meat on the fire; the visitors would be hungry. Abraham went out to greet them. What handsome men they were. They reminded him of angels; they only needed wings.

"Welcome. Welcome to my encampment."

He ushered the visitors into his tent, begging them to sit on the softest, newest rugs. Abraham himself served them fresh milk, cheese and the best meat, hot from the spit.

"We have great news for you," said one of the men. "The Lord God says that within a year your wife Sarah will have a baby, a son."

Kneading dough outside the tent, Sarah overheard the strangers. She had to suppress a laugh. She was old now, too old to bear children. How could she have a child? No, now she could only help to look after her servants' children.

But God had other plans. Nine months later, as the three mysterious visitors had predicted, Sarah gave birth to a baby boy. She and Abraham called him Isaac. The boy grew up to be a healthy, good-looking lad. His parents' servants taught him to ride donkeys and camels and showed him how to hunt and make fire with sticks. His mother and father taught him to pray and to obey God and all his wishes.

But one night, while Abraham was looking up at the stars, feeling happy that his son was doing so well, he heard the voice of God again.

"Abraham, I want you to take Isaac to the land of Moriah, to a mountain of my choosing. There, I want you to build an altar and sacrifice him to me."

Abraham reeled. What? Kill Isaac – his only son, whom he loved with all his heart?

God's voice came again, echoing through the trees.

"Obey me, Abraham, without question and I shall make you the father of a great nation."

Abraham knew there was no arguing with God. He chose two servants to accompany Isaac and himself and, early the next morning, they left camp.

"Say goodbye to your mother, Isaac."

Abraham's heart was breaking as he said the words. When they reached the foot of the mountain God had chosen, he told the servants to put up tents.

"Isaac and I are going further up the mountain to offer sacrifice."

The servants handed them some wood and a brazier of hot coals. Abraham made sure he had a knife tucked under his sash, the old knife he used to slaughter the lambs that he sacrificed to God. Isaac put the wood on his back, proud that he could carry it without help.

As they scrambled over the rocks, Isaac said, "Father, we have wood and fire, but where is the lamb we are going to sacrifice?"

"God will provide it, my son."

At last they came to a spot where the wind blew clear across the mountain. It was the perfect place. The breeze would carry the smoke of the sacrifice straight up to heaven. Father and son built an altar using the stones they found scattered on the mountainside. When it was ready, they piled it high with wood. Abraham blew on the embers in the brazier to keep them alight. Soon he would need them to set fire to the wood. He and his son were getting tired now. Isaac was yawning; he was half asleep.

"Forgive me, my son," whispered Abraham. Working quickly, he wrapped the strong rope around his sleepy son and tied it fast.

Isaac looked up, his face fuddled with tiredness, blinking at his father.

"Father. What are you doing?"

"Do not ask questions, my son."

"Am I to be sacrificed, Father? Am I the lamb?"

"We cannot disobey God, my son."

Fighting back the tears, Abraham lifted his son and placed him on the altar. The lad was too weak to wriggle or resist. Perhaps God had made him sleepy on purpose, to dull the pain of the knife. He looked so young, so vulnerable, lying on the wood like a baby in a manger. How could God ask this of Abraham? Who was going to give him as many descendants as stars in the heavens now? He tried hard to suppress his rebellious thoughts. He had to obey God – obey him without question. Abraham had to believe in God and his promises even when he did not understand what God was planning.

He took the knife from under his sash, its blade dull and rusted. Abraham steadied his trembling hand and raised the knife high in the air, ready to strike.

"Goodbye, my son. God, accept my humble offering."

There was a whoosh behind him, a rush of wind that nearly blew him off his feet. Something gripped his arm and held it fast.

"Do not hurt the child."

It was the angel of the Lord.

"Now God knows that you fear him,

because you have not kept back your only son from him. There is no need for the killing."

Abraham dropped the knife on the rocky ground. Tears of gratitude and relief welled in his eyes. God had not meant him to kill his only son after all, he was only testing him. Abraham untied Isaac and helped him down from the altar, hugging him to his chest. Nearby, he heard an angry snort and looked up to see a ram caught in a tree by its horns. He would sacrifice the ram instead of his son. He and Isaac would sacrifice it together.

The angel of the Lord swooped up above them, lighting up the sky with his brilliance and spoke for the Lord.

"Because you have obeyed me, Abraham, I shall keep my promise to you. You shall have as many descendants as there are stars in the heavens, or grains of sand on the beach. They will honour you as their father."

Abraham and Isaac looked up from their altar, where the wood was catching fire. The sky was teeming with stars, twinkling and shining in the velvety darkness. There were so many, no one could possibly begin to count them. Abraham was going to be the father of a great nation indeed.

A Bride for Isaac

*Before he had finished speaking, there was
Rebekah . . . coming out with her water-jar on her
shoulder. The girl was very fair to look upon.*

GENESIS 24:15-16

Abraham was very old now, so old that he could not walk without the help of his trusted servant. One evening, the two were enjoying a cool stroll among the date palms.

"It is time Isaac got married," said Abraham. "I want you to go back to Haran, the distant city where my people come from, and I want you to find a Hebrew bride for him there."

"Master, would it not be better for him to find a wife here in Canaan?" said the trusted servant, helping him to sit down on a rock. "After all, we are settled here. This is Isaac's home."

"I promised Sarah that he would marry one of our own people," said Abraham, "a woman who believes in God, not someone who worships idols. It was her last wish before she died."

So the trusted servant took ten camels and presents for Isaac's intended bride and her family. He took men with him who could ride camels, cook food on open fires and fight with bandits in the desert, should they happen upon them. The party set out across the desert, crossing the great plain of Paddan Aram, until they came to a well on the outskirts of Haran. It was late afternoon, the time when the local women came out to fill their pitchers with water.

The servant closed his eyes and prayed to God.

"Lord," he said, "help me to find the right wife for my master's son. I shall ask one of the young women at the well to let me drink from her pitcher. If she accepts and also fetches water for my camels, let her be the one you have chosen as the bride for Isaac."

Before he had finished speaking, a cool shadow fell across his face. Standing before the old servant was a beautiful young woman.

"Is anything the matter, traveller?"

"I have travelled far and my throat is parched. Would you give me some water from your pitcher, please?"

The young woman smiled a gentle smile full of kindness.

"Of course. And I'll fetch water for your camels and companions too. They look as parched as you."

The servant drank deeply, then the young woman drew more water and filled the camels' trough. The trusted servant fumbled in his pocket for the jewellery Abraham had given him: two golden bracelets and a nose ring, studded with little jewels.

"You have been extremely kind to us," he said to the young woman, fastening the bracelets around her wrist. "Please tell me who your father is and whether he would give us a room for the night in his house?"

"My name is Rebekah," replied the girl, staring at the golden bracelets on her wrist. She had often helped travellers at the well, but no one had rewarded her like this before. Were these people ambassadors of a king or queen, or the servants of a rich nomad in the desert? "My father is Bethuel, son of Nahor and Milcah. We have plenty of space for your men and camels. Please, follow me."

Bethuel, son of Nahor and Milcah, was Abraham's own nephew. God had directed the servant straight to his master's family.

The servant's men were rousing the camels to their feet when a young man came running to meet them.

"Rebekah, your mother is waiting for you at home."

"These travellers need shelter for the night, brother Laban," Rebekah said. "I have said they may stay with us."

"Sir," said the trusted servant, "we are in the employ of your great uncle, Abraham. God has blessed him and he is now a very rich and respected man in the land of Canaan. He has sent me here on urgent business."

Laban caught sight of the bracelets on Rebekah's wrist and the jewelled nose ring. Only a very wealthy man could afford to give presents like that. Had Great Uncle Abraham really become so rich?

"Come with me," he said, and the little caravan followed him up the road to a house with a flat roof, its doors standing wide open to catch the evening breeze.

Seeing travellers outside, the women of the house started cooking right away. It would not do to leave visitors hungry.

Laban fetched help and the camels were taken away to be given food, water and rest.

Before long, the smell of cooking meat wafted through the house. Bethuel and his wife made the trusted servant welcome. They were impressed by how devoted the old servant was to his master. They offered him food

"Daughter,' said Bethuel, "do you want to be Isaac's wife?"

Rebekah nodded, smiling. "It is God's will, Father. Who am I to object?"

So her parents gave her their blessing and she called her own maid servants and asked them to pack her clothes and belongings.

In the morning, the little caravan set

but the old servant would not touch a morsel, not a crumb, before he had finished his business. He told them what he had come for and how he'd prayed to God to help him find the right wife for Isaac.

"If God chose Rebekah himself, who are we to stand in his way?" said Bethuel. "Take my daughter to Canaan and let her become Isaac's wife."

Just then Rebekah came in.

out from Haran on the long journey across the great desert. Rebekah, seated on a camel, turned to bid her parents farewell. She had never set foot outside the city before, she had never gone further than the traveller's well, but Rebekah wasn't scared. Something inside told her that Isaac would make her very happy, that he would love and respect her.

She would be proud to be his wife.

Jacob and Esau

*"See, I am old; I do not know the day of my death.
Now then, take your weapons, your quiver and your bow,
and go out to the field and hunt game for me."*

GENESIS 27:2–3

Isaac and Rebekah had twin sons – Jacob and Esau. Esau was the eldest, born only a few minutes before Jacob. Esau grew to be hairy and well-muscled, liking nothing better than hunting wild animals. His father was very proud of him and often boasted to friends that he made the best stews in Canaan.

Jacob, on the other hand, had smooth skin that burnt easily in the sun. His job was to help his father look after the flocks but he preferred to stay at home in the shade, grinding corn or churning butter for his mother. He was Rebekah's favourite.

One day, when Isaac was very old and almost blind, he called Esau to him.

"Make me one of your famous spicy stews and I will give you the blessing a father gives his first son."

Esau went to fetch his bow and arrow right away. With the father's blessing to the eldest son would come

everything Isaac owned: his tents, his herds, his slaves, his crops. He would become the head of the family when Isaac died.

"I'll catch a deer," thought Esau. "My father likes venison best."

But Rebekah, spinning wool outside the tent, had overheard Isaac and Esau. She was not pleased. With his father's blessing, Esau would also take on the responsibility of the family, when Isaac died. He would have to look after the herdsmen and their families, the field workers and the servants. He would have to make sure that the family traditions, its customs and its belief in the one true God, would be continued. Esau had never shown the slightest bit of interest in family tradition. He'd even married two women from a different culture, who worshipped other gods, false gods. No, Rebekah had to make sure the family was protected…

Calling Jacob from his tent, she ordered him to kill two young goats from the best flock in the fields. While he was doing that, she stoked the fire, chopped wild onions and pounded spices in an earthenware bowl. Jacob returned with the meat on a platter. Together they made a thick and delicious stew.

"Who is it for?" asked Jacob. "Are we expecting visitors?"

"Sssh," said his mother. "Go and fetch me Esau's cloak, the one he uses when it gets cold in winter."

"But mother…" protested Jacob.

"Do as I say."

The boy fetched the cloak from the tent. It felt soft in his hands; the fur smelt of the field and the spicy bushes that grew there.

"Put it on."

"But Esau won't be pleased, mother."

"This is not the time for arguing, son." Jacob wrapped the cloak around himself. His mother took the hairy skins of the goats he'd killed for the stew and tucked them around Jacob's neck and inside the sleeves of his robe.

"Mother, what are you up to?"

Rebekah smiled. "Now your arms feel as hairy as Esau's. You smell like him, too." She sniffed the cloak.

"Mmmm, wild grass and spices." She ladled stew into Isaac's bowl and thrust bread into Jacob's hand.

"Your father promised Esau his blessing today, but I want you to have it. You are better at caring for this family than he is. Quick, take your father this stew before your brother returns."

"But what if Father finds out I'm not Esau and thinks I'm insulting him? You know how fond he is of Esau."

"Then I shall bear the brunt of his curse," said Rebekah, pushing Jacob towards his father's tent.

The boy entered, his eyes straining to see in the gloom. Isaac was resting on a couch, a blanket over his wrinkled feet.

"Esau, is that you?"

"Yes, Father."

"You sound like Jacob."

"It is Esau, Father."

Jacob moved closer with the bowl of stew and his father placed his gnarled hands on his arms.

"You sound like Jacob, but your arms are hairy like Esau's. Are you really my son Esau?"

"Yes, Father."

"You smell like Esau. That hunter's cloak. I can smell wild grass and spices.

Have you been hunting for wild goat?"

"Yes, Father," said Jacob, placing the warm bowl in his father's lap.

"This stew smells good – spicy, just how I like it."

He dipped the bread in and tasted it.

"It is good. You make the best stew in Canaan, Esau."

Isaac took a long time to eat it, savouring every morsel. Jacob's heart beat loudly in his chest. What if Esau came back before his father had finished eating? Would there be a fight? Would Isaac curse him?

"This is good, my son. Kiss me and I shall bless you."

Jacob did as his father asked, aware that his mother was standing outside the tent, watching everything. Isaac sniffed Esau's cloak again.

"The pleasant smell of my son is like the smell of a field that the Lord has blessed. May God give you dew from heaven and make all your fields fertile. May you rule over all your relatives and may all the family accept you as their leader. Let all those who curse you be cursed and all those who bless you be blessed."

"Thank you, Father." Jacob stood up and removed the bowl from his father's lap. His mother beckoned to him, and he left the tent, removing Esau's heavy cloak from his shoulders.

"Esau is back from the hunt. Hide, quick! I'll tell you when to come back."

As Jacob fled, slipping through the trees behind the tent, Esau approached, carrying a deer. He cooked it quickly and skilfully, adding wine and garlic.

"Father, sit up and eat."

"Who's that?"

"It's Esau. I have made this delicious venison stew for you."

"But you've already fed me, Esau. You gave me stewed goat."

Esau put down the bowl. "That can't have been me, Father. I have been out hunting deer."

Isaac started shaking with anger. He realised he'd been tricked, deceived.

Now that Esau was in the tent, he could tell that his voice was much rougher than that of… Jacob.

"I've already given the blessing to your brother."

"What?"

"He stole your blessing. Your younger brother, Jacob, stole your blessing."

Now it was Esau's turn to start shaking. He hurled the stew to the ground, smashing the bowl to pieces.

"Give me your blessing, Father. I am the eldest. I have the right to it."

"You have, my son, but there is nothing I can do now. Once a blessing is given, no one can take it back."

Esau reeled. Now his brother would be the head of the family. When Isaac died he would make all the decisions, instruct the workers and the servants and choose wives for his relatives. He, Esau, would be his own brother's slave, forced to be at his beck and call for the rest of his life. Unless, unless…

"I shall kill him," roared Esau. "I shall squeeze the life out of him with my bare hands. Then I shall be the head of the family, as is my right, my God-given right."

Esau sank to his knees, wretched, defeated, the tears of frustration streaming down his face.

In the grove behind the tents, Jacob heard his brother's roar. What could he do now? He couldn't go back to his tent or the fields – Esau would find him.

Rebekah appeared with a bundle in her hands.

"You must escape to the city of Haran. It's too far away for Esau to follow you there. My brother, Laban, keeps his flocks outside the city walls. He'll take care of you until I send word that you can come home again."

Jacob kissed her and hugged her close.

"Laban has two daughters, they are your cousins. Perhaps you can marry one of them?" she said.

"Perhaps, Mother."

Jacob could hear his brother crashing through the trees, looking for him. Did Esau have his bow and arrow with him? Nothing was beyond his brother when he was angry.

"Goodbye Mother." One last kiss, one last hug, and Rebekah's favourite son was gone, running through the trees, swallowed by the gathering night.

"Goodbye, my son. God look after you and bless you." And with that, she turned back to the tent, to Isaac, to Esau. She was going to need all her courage in the next few days.

Jacob and the Stranger

And he was afraid, and said,
"How awesome is this place! This is none other than
the house of God, and this is the gate of heaven."

GENESIS 28:17

Jacob ran through the trees, further and further away from his family's tents, his fields, everything he loved and held dear. For a while he kept turning, expecting his brother Esau to be behind him. But no one came, no sharp arrows were fired in his direction. At sundown he stopped in a clearing. He found a smooth stone to use as a pillow and patted down a stretch of

rough grass for a bed. Exhausted, he lay down. How life had changed in just one day. He had inherited all his father's wealth and then he had lost everything. What was the use of having the first son's blessing if you were too afraid to go home and use it?

At last Jacob fell asleep. Towards morning he had a vivid dream: the clouds in the sky parted to reveal a staircase rising up into the stars. Angels, their wings folded neatly behind their backs, were going up and down the steps. There were so many of them, hundreds, thousands even.

"*I am the God of Isaac, your father and Abraham, your grandfather,*" whispered a voice in Jacob's mind. "*I am your God, too. All this land on which you are lying will be yours. It will be filled with your children and your children's children. They will be as many as the specks of dust on this earth. Remember, I shall be with you until my promise has come true.*"

Jacob woke with a start, his eyes wide open. The staircase to heaven had vanished. He stood the stone he had been using as a pillow on its side, a sign that he was making a pact with God.

"I will honour you as my God too," he promised, pouring oil on the stone from the flask his mother had packed for him. "But please, help me return home safely."

The agreement made, Jacob continued on his journey. For weeks, months, he walked through towns, cities, deserts and oases, until one day he came to the town of Haran, its walls rising high against the blue sky. Travellers on camels and donkeys jostled to get through the gates, which the guards had just opened. In the fields outside were mud houses shaped like beehives and tents where the herdsmen and the nomads lived.

Jacob stopped at a well to quench his thirst.

"Do you know Laban?" he asked the shepherds drawing water for their cattle.

"We work for him," they said. "All these animals belong to him. Here comes his daughter Rachel to fetch water for the lambs."

Jacob looked up to see a young woman coming down the road, a water jug on her shoulder. He had never seen anyone so graceful, so beautiful, in all his life. Rachel smiled and Jacob's heart started pounding in his chest.

"I am your cousin," he said shyly.

"My cousin?"

He nodded. "From Beersheba in Canaan."

A smile spread across Rachel's face. "You must be Esau. We have heard that you are very strong."

"No, I am Jacob, his younger brother."

"Welcome to Haran, cousin."

Jacob just couldn't resist that smile any longer. He leaned forward and kissed Rachel on the lips. That night, after a meal in Laban's tent, he spoke to his uncle.

"I love Rachel. It's love at first sight. Will you let me marry her?"

Laban nodded, "But grooms usually bring generous gifts with them, to add to the families riches. Have you brought anything?"

"Nothing," admitted Jacob. "But I am willing to work for free instead. I am a good shepherd. Your flocks will prosper under my care."

"Very well," agreed Laban. "You will work for me for seven years, then I will allow you to marry Rachel."

Seven years passed like a dream, a dream in which Jacob's love for Rachel grew stronger and stronger. Under Jacob's care, Laban's flocks multiplied. He now had so many sheep he could hardly count them. Soon it was time for Jacob to marry Rachel and take her back to his people in Canaan. But Laban, worried about losing his best shepherd, hatched a plan…

On the day of the wedding, delicious food was served. The wine flowed. The family and their guests danced until it got dark and the gates of Haran closed for the night. Jacob and Laban shook hands over the deal. Jacob was now married; Laban was his father-in-law. As the moon rose, Jacob's bride was shown into his tent, swathed in veils, her face hidden in shadows. It was only in the morning that Jacob realised he'd been tricked. The woman he had married, had shaken hands on, wasn't Rachel. It was Leah, her older sister, the plain one that nobody wanted.

"It is our custom to marry the older sister first," explained Laban. "You can marry Rachel next week, if you work for me for seven more years."

Jacob was furious, disappointed and hurt. But there was nothing he could do about Leah – she was officially his wife now. So he agreed to work for another seven years. His beloved Rachel soon became his wife and only one bitter disappointment that tinged their love with sadness. Rachel could not become pregnant.

Wanting heirs, Jacob turned to her slave Bilhah, Leah, and Zilpah, Leah's maidservant. Between them, the three women gave him eleven children: Dinah, a girl, and Reuben, Simeon, Levi, Judah, Dan, Naphtali, Gad, Asher, Issachar and Zebulun, all boys. Then, joy of joys, Rachel became pregnant too. She had a son called Joseph.

Life was perfect for Jacob now. Laban had given him his own flocks and, with the help of God, his sheep and goats, his bulls, cows and camels had multiplied in number. He was rich, respected and loved. It was time to go back home to Canaan, to see his father and mother and show them all the wealth he now possessed. It was time to heal the rift with Esau.

On the way home, Jacob had another dream. He woke up to find himself wrestling with a stranger. For hours they struggled, the man trying to beat Jacob to the ground, Jacob trying to set himself free. Who was this man? Jacob wondered. When the sun rose and revealed the stranger's face, he realised it was someone from heaven, an angel perhaps, a messenger sent to him by God.

"It's morning," said the stranger, "and I still haven't won. Let me go."

"Only if you give me a blessing," answered Jacob, tightening his grip on the stranger's shoulder.

"What is your name?" asked the angel.

"I am Jacob, son of Isaac, grandson of Abraham."

"You have struggled with God and won," said the stranger. "From now on you shall be known as Israel, and your descendants as the Children of Israel." And he raised his hands in blessing and was gone.

The sun had risen now, filling the air with golden light. Jacob limped after his wives and servants, whom he'd sent ahead with gifts for Esau. The angel had dealt him a blow on the hip, throwing it out of joint. Esau was waiting on the crest of a hill, his arms open to receive his long-lost brother.

The two embraced, patting each other on the back. "I missed you," said Jacob. "Brother, forgive me."

Jacob's children, wives and servants crowded around Esau, touching their heads as a sign of respect.

"Welcome back to Canaan," said Esau, tears of forgiveness and joy running down his face.

"Welcome home, Brother."

Joseph and his Dreams

*When his brothers saw that their father
loved him more than all his brothers, they hated him,
and could not speak peaceably to him.*

GENESIS 37:4

Rachel had a second son before she died: Benjamin, the youngest in the family. Jacob loved him with all his heart but, still, his favourite son remained Rachel's firstborn, Joseph. He did not do much to hide the fact either. While the the other brothers had to make do with threadbare tunics, even in winter, Jacob bought Joseph a thick coat with full sleeves and long, colourful stripes.

"I wouldn't want my favourite son to catch cold while he's looking after the sheep," he said to his friends.

Joseph's brothers seethed with anger and jealousy, but they said nothing. Their father was getting old and they did not want to upset him. Then one day, Jacob called them all back from the hills where they were tending the flocks. He wanted them to help harvest the fields near the tents.

"I had a dream about harvests," said Joseph to his brothers as they all sat eating in Jacob's tent. "I dreamt we each had a sheaf standing in the field. Mine was right in the middle and yours all turned and bowed to mine."

"Be quiet," said Reuben. "Sheaves of corn don't bow to anyone."

"I had an even better dream," continued Joseph, ignoring his eldest brother and the angry looks from the rest. "I saw eleven stars in the sky, and they all twinkled and bowed to me."

The brothers nearly choked on their stew. Was Joseph telling the truth or was he making this up? They'd all heard that dreams had secret meanings. Were they the eleven sheaves and stars? Were they really going to bow to Joseph, their father's pet, and recognise him as their leader?

A few days later, the elder brothers left in search of grazing land for their flocks. Jacob, wanting to know where they were going to camp, sent Joseph after them. The brothers saw him coming on foot, his bag bumping against his hip.

"Here comes Father's favourite," sneered Dan.

"Wearing his lovely winter coat," added Asher.

The brothers were shivering in the cold and the sight of Joseph's warm clothes made them green with envy.

"Let's kill the spoilt brat," said one of them.

"Yes, let's drown him in a well!"

"Don't be foolish," argued Reuben. "Throw him in a dry well. It'll give him a good scare and stop him boasting about his dreams. But don't soil your hands with his blood. He is not a criminal."

"A twinkling star, eh? Let's see you reach for the heavens now."

In the distance there was a jangle of bells. The brothers looked up to see a caravan wending its way across the plain. The camels were piled high with bundles of goods, wicker baskets and bolts of rare cloth. Behind them, tied up in chains, tottered a line of slaves, bought in markets along the trade route.

"Let's sell Joseph," suggested Judah. "He won't make a very good slave but it'll teach him some humility."

Before he knew it, Joseph was plucked out of the well and handed over to the traders. With a screech of metal, a chain was clamped around his right foot.

He had been sold to Ishmaelite merchants for twenty shekels. The merchants handed over the money and

When Joseph drew near, his brothers leapt on him and tore off his precious coat. Before he could speak, they threw him down a dry well, where he landed on soft sand.

"There, idiot. Why don't you tell us your dreams now?"

Joseph was forced to follow the caravan, stumbling over the rough ground. Behind him, one of his brothers picked up the torn coat.

"We'll dip his coat in goat's blood," Judah said, "and tell father that

Joseph was eaten by wild animals…"

The traders took Joseph to Egypt, where he was sold along with the cloth and the spices. His new master was a captain called Potiphar, who knew Pharaoh personally. Joseph did well in his house. Despite a tendency to boast, he was a good worker and was soon made the head of the household.

Joseph's good luck did not last.

"We heard that you interpret dreams, Joseph. We both had a dream last night – about Pharaoh."

"What did you dream?" asked Joseph.

The two prisoners described their dreams and Joseph told them what the dreams foretold: the first prisoner was going to be released, to become the king's servant again, but the second prisoner was destined for the gallows.

Potiphar's wife, taking a liking to Joseph, tried to seduce him.

When he rejected her, she lied to Potiphar, telling him that Joseph had offended her. Joseph found himself in chains again, not as a slave this time, but in prison, as a common criminal. He might have spent the rest of his life there, forgotten by everyone, had he not been approached by two prisoners.

All happened as Joseph had predicted and the first prisoner found himself close to Pharoah once again.

Two years later, as this servant was pouring wine for the king, Pharaoh told him, "I had two dreams last night but no one can tell me what they mean, not even the court magicians."

The servant remembered Joseph in his cell and had him summoned.

"I dreamt I saw seven fat cows come out of the Nile," said Pharaoh to Joseph. "They started to gobble up the grass. Behind them came seven other cows, but these were thin, their ribs showing through their hides. Even though they gobbled up the fat cows, they still remained thin."

"My second dream was about ears of corn. The first seven were fat and full of grain, but seven thin ones sprouted out of the ground and ate them up."

"Both your dreams have the same meaning," explained Joseph. "The next seven years are going to be very good for Egypt. There will be great harvests. But the seven years after that will be terrible. The Nile flood will not bring prosperity and people will starve. You should choose someone to look after the country's grain, Your Majesty. If the farmers put by enough corn in the seven years of plenty, there should be enough to last Egypt through the seven years of famine."

The king was so impressed with Joseph's words that he put him in charge of storing Egypt's grain. Joseph's tattered clothes were replaced with luxurious tunics. He was given a room in the palace and a horse and chariot of his own.

During the years of famine he did not let Pharaoh down. Even though the harvests were a disaster, there was still plenty of food for everyone in the land.

News of Egypt's store of corn attracted merchants from all over the world. They came to Joseph begging, clamouring, to buy grain for their starving people back home. The famine, it seemed, had affected many countries. And so it was that one day Joseph saw his ten elder brothers waiting in line for grain. They did not recognise this grown-up Joseph, dressed in fine clothes.

"Are you really here to buy grain?" Joseph asked, "or are you spies?"

"We are not spies," said the brothers, bowing before him.

Joseph remembered his dreams.

The sheaves of corn. The stars bowing down in front of him, just as his brothers were bowing now. His dreams had come true after all.

"I think you are spies."

"No! We are honest men come to buy food for our families, for our father and our youngest brother who has stayed back at home with him."

Joseph knew they were referring to Benjamin. Did they hate him too, because he was the son of Rachel, Jacob's favourite wife? He would soon find out…

"I don't believe you," he said. "You have no father waiting at home. There is no brother."

"But it's true. Our youngest brother is called Benjamin."

"Very well, then, prove it to me. Go and fetch Benjamin from your homeland. I will keep one of you here." He pointed to Simeon. "Guards, tie that one up and throw him in prison."

Then he was gone, hiding his face with his hands so that his brothers could not see he was crying. The brothers returned home with the grain but without Simeon.

"I am indeed very unlucky," said Jacob. "First I lose Joseph, then Simeon, and now you want to take Benjamin. No, I will not let him go."

But soon all the grain was eaten and the sacks were empty. The brothers had no choice but to go back to Egypt, this time with Benjamin. Joseph received them with open arms. He filled their sacks with grain, refusing to take money for it. The guards let Simeon out of prison so that he could join his brothers for dinner. While they were eating,

Joseph ordered one of the servants to hide his cup in Benjamin's pack.

"Now I shall find out if my brothers will betray Benjamin as they betrayed me," he thought.

After the meal, the brothers hurried to the stables, where they hoisted their sacks of grain on to their donkey's backs. They were eager to get back home and feed their families.

"Wait," called Joseph. "One of you has stolen my silver cup."

The guards started searching, tearing open sacks, running their knives through each bundle. They found Joseph's silver goblet hidden at the bottom of Benjamin's pack.

"Throw that filthy thief in prison," spat Joseph.

"No! Imprison me!"

"Keep me!"

The brothers kneeled before Joseph, begging for Benjamin's release and offering themselves.

"He is only young. He couldn't have stolen your cup. What would a young boy do with such a thing in his father's tent? We can't go back home without him. It would break our father's heart."

Joseph knew by the way they were talking that they had mended their ways. Every one of them was ready to give up his freedom for Benjamin's. Tears welled in his eyes as he removed his crown.

"Brothers, do you not recognise me? I am Joseph, your brother. I did not die a slave, I am alive and prosperous."

The brothers stood up in confusion. Was this man in front of them really Joseph? Was their brother really still alive?

"I forgive you for what you have done to me," said Joseph, "because God meant me to come to Egypt and save lives."

Then his brothers recognised Joseph and they gathered around him, hugging him close. That very same day, Joseph sent for his father. Jacob came to Egypt, carried in a chariot made of pure gold. Father and son were reunited at last, in a country where they could all prosper, even in the remaining years of famine.

Moses in the Bulrushes

*When she could hide him no longer she got
a papyrus basket for him, and . . . she put the child in it
and placed it among the reeds on the bank of the river.*

EXODUS 2:3

Joseph and his brothers lived long, prosperous lives in Egypt. Pharaoh gave them a part of the country to use as their own, a fertile region called Goshen. But time passed and Joseph and his eleven brothers died, leaving behind them twelve huge families – twelve tribes. Over hundreds of years the twelve tribes grew into a whole nation. Then, quite unexpectedly, something happened which was to affect the life of every Israelite. A new king came to the throne, one who wanted to rule over an empire that would stretch over many countries. This king did not like the Israelites.

In fact, he hated them. He considered them to be a disgusting part of his great kingdom.

"They refuse to bow down to Egyptian gods," Pharoah grumbled to his ministers. "They worship only one god, their god. If there is ever a war, they will side with the enemy. I want them thinned out, like weeds in a garden."

The ministers hatched a plan. The king was building a new city. The Israelites would be made to work on it, producing bricks and building temples. Many of them were not used to such hard work. Surely slave-labour would finish off a lot of them?

So life changed dramatically for Joseph's descendants. Instead of wealthy shepherds, they were now slaves, working from dawn until well after dusk. Many died in accidents, by the crack of a soldier's whip or through thirst and exhaustion. But not enough of them to set Pharaoh's mind at rest.

"The Israelites are still growing in number. There are more and more of them every day," he said to his generals. "Order the soldiers to drown every one of their newborn sons in the Nile. That way there will be no men to father new Israelite babies."

Pharaoh's soldiers had no choice but to carry out his horrific plans. Every time an Israelite baby was born, they would come knocking at the door, forcing their way into the house. If the newborn was a girl, they left her in her mother's arms. But if they found a boy, he was roughly bundled out of the hut, down to the river. Sometimes the night in Goshen echoed with the wails of drowning babies and the screams of heart-broken mothers.

"This is unjust," said a young mother from the tribe of Levi. "We have done nothing to deserve this."

The young woman was expecting a child, perhaps a boy who would help his father with the flocks when he grew up. She had no intention of losing him. So she asked her daughter, Miriam, to fetch bulrushes from the river. Together they wove a huge basket with a lid that fitted snugly. When it was ready, they lined it with tar so that water would not seep into it.

"What is it for, mother?"

"You'll see, Miriam," said her mother, hiding the new basket among their sacks of grain.

When the child was born, the young woman made no fuss. Not one single cry passed her lips. Only the midwife who came to help knew about the birth. The child was a boy, healthy and strong, with a thick tuft of hair on his head.

"Please, don't give us away," the mother begged the midwife. "This Israelite boy is going to live."

"Your secret is safe with me," vowed the midwife. And she kept her word. No soldiers came knocking at the door, no neighbours called with gifts. For three months, Miriam and her mother managed to keep their baby safe. But soon his loud cries could be heard by the neighbours.

"I'm sure I heard a boy crying," said the woman who lived in the hut across the track. "It sounded just like my Caleb when he was little."

"It's time to use the basket," said Miriam's mother.

They fetched it and put the baby inside.

That night, almost invisible in the cloudy gloom, they hurried to the River Nile, where their washing still hung drying on the reeds. Miriam's mother set the basket on the water.

"Goodbye, my little one," she whispered, pushing the basket out into the current. "May God watch over you and bless you."

The current picked up the basket and carried it down river, bobbing up and down. Miriam ran along the bank after it, eager to see where it would stop. It was dawn when the basket finally snagged on a reed and stopped among the bulrushes. Miriam looked around her. They were very close to Pharaoh's palace. Through the reeds, she could see a terrace filled with birdcages.

"Nurse, fetch my linen, quick."

It was the princess, Pharaoh's daughter, coming out for her early morning bathe.

"Nurse, did you bring my perfume?"

"Yes, Mistress."

The princess waded into the river, gasping as the cold water hit her legs.

"Nurse, what's that in the reeds? Is it a sleeping swan?"

The nurse waded into the water too,

frowning at the chill of the Nile at dawn.

"No, it seems to be a basket of some sort, mistress."

The princess was intrigued. This was like having an unexpected present, a gift from a visiting ambassador.

"Open the lid. Let's see what's inside."

"Careful, Princess, there might be something dangerous in there."

The nurse reached out and pulled the basket to the bank. She opened it and there was the baby, wrapped up tight against the chill of the morning.

"It must be an Israelite boy," gasped the princess. "Look at him, poor thing, he's crying from the cold. Nurse, fetch me a blanket."

"But Princess…" began the nurse.

"Do as I say," snapped the princess. What a wonderful surprise to find a child in a basket, floating on the river. And such a pretty boy too. He had big eyes and a shock of hair on his head.

"I mean to keep him," said the princess. "I'll raise him as my own. The gods have sent me this child, for a reason I do not yet know."

"But Princess, all Israelite boys are supposed to be dead. His mother must have put him in the basket hoping to save him."

"And he will be saved," replied the princess. "No one need know he is an Israelite. He will be an Egyptian prince, brought up as my own child.

You will be in great trouble if you tell anyone about what has happened here this morning."

The nurse realised it was useless to protest. The princess was very stubborn. Once she made a decision, no one could ever change her mind.

"Perhaps we could find an Israelite wet nurse to feed him and take care of him?" she said. "So many mothers have lost their babies, it shouldn't be hard."

"Please Your Majesty, I know of someone who will take care of that child," piped up a voice in the reeds. It was Miriam. She had been hiding, watching everything.

"Please fetch her," said the princess. "And be discreet. You shall lose your head if word of this gets out."

Miriam ran to fetch a wet nurse – her mother. The two hurried to the palace, tucking their hair into their scarves as they ran.

"Please look after this child for me," ordered the princess, handing Miriam's mother the child, now swathed in fine linen sheets. "I will pay you well."

Miriam's mother clasped her son tightly to her chest. He was alive, her son was safe. And now he was going to be a prince.

"Have you a name for him, Your Majesty?" she asked.

"Yes," said the princess. "I have decided to call him Moses."

Moses and the Burning Bush

There the angel of the Lord appeared to him in a flame of fire out of a bush; he looked, and the bush was blazing, yet it was not consumed.

EXODUS 3:2

When Moses was three years old, it was time for his mother to take him back to the palace. The princess, unable to have children of her own, spoilt him, bringing him up as an Egyptian prince. He learnt to write, to ride chariots across the desert and to hunt for wild snakes with a golden spear. His clothes were the finest in the land: best quality cloaks and flawless linen tunics, brightly-coloured with beautiful jewelled collars. Every day, slaves shaved his skin until it was smooth; they cut his hair and sprinkled him with rare perfume. No other prince was as handsome as Moses.

Except Moses did not feel like a prince. He felt different from all the other young men, the sons of the king's concubines, who lived in the palace. Out strolling the streets, he often wondered why some people were wealthy while others lived in harsh conditions that made their lives a misery. He didn't think it was just by luck that a few lived in luxury while others made do with mud huts and tents infested with vermin and disease. Especially the Israelites. They seemed to have it worse than anyone else in Egypt. As he walked, he wondered why that was.

Then one day he discovered a startling secret: "You are an Israelite yourself," whispered the old nurse. "It's true. Your mother, the princess, found you in the river. I plucked you out myself."

Now Moses understood why he felt out of place in the palace. He did not belong there. He belonged with his people, in Goshen. But did he want to spend his life making bricks and building temples? Did he want to be a slave?

He had been brought up in privilege and luxury. He had never known anything else. This was a hard decision to make.

One morning, steering his chariot through the streets of Goshen, Moses heard the crack of a whip. He pulled on the horse's reins, halting the chariot to see what was going on. The noise was coming from an Egyptian overseer, beating an Israelite slave who had dropped his water jug on the way back from the well.

"I told you to be careful with the water jug, you animal!" shouted the overseer, his face red with anger as he brought the whip down on the Israelite's back.

Moses was furious. How could the overseer treat another human being that way over a water jug? Quickly, Moses stepped down from his chariot. The Israelite slave, mistaking him for another Egyptian who would no doubt join in the beating, scrambled to his feet and ran away.

"Sir," the overseer bowed.

That was the last word he ever said. Moses ran him through with his spear and the overseer fell to the ground. Bundling the man's body into the chariot, Moses rode out into the desert and buried him in the sand. For a while Moses thought nobody had witnessed the crime. But only the next day, while he was trying to stop two Israelites from fighting, he heard someone shout.

"Are you going to kill those men too, Sir, just as you killed that Egyptian overseer yesterday?"

Moses realised he had been seen. There was not a moment to lose. He had to escape. Not to the palace – Pharoah would have him arrested if he went there – but somewhere far away, somewhere safe.

Exchanging his tunic for a simple robe, Moses took one of the horses from his chariot and fled Egypt. Thundering across the desert, he did not care which direction the horse took him in. After a few hours, Moses found himself marvelling at how much his life had changed in just one day. Only this morning he had been a prince, he had been among the most wealthy people in Egypt. Now he was a fugitive, running from the law. What did life have in store for him?

In the desert, Moses met a Midianite family: a father called Jethro and his seven daughters. The Midianites were nomads, like Moses's ancestors. They wandered around the desert, herding their flocks. Jethro offered Moses work looking after their sheep and goats. It would be his job to take them into the hills when the desert got too dry. Moses accepted the kind offer. After a while, he married one of the seven sisters, Zipporah, who gave him two sons, Gershom and Eliezer. At last Moses felt like he fitted in. Life was good.

But God had plans for Moses – big plans that didn't involve looking after sheep or marking out waterholes. One day, the prince-turned-shepherd was tending his flock on a mountain – a forbidding place called Mount Horeb – when he noticed a burning bush. Curious, he saw that the flames were not harming the plant, but were merely rising out of it.

Suddenly, a voice echoed out of the burning bush.

"I am the God of your ancestors. The God of Abraham and Isaac, the God of Jacob. Do not come closer, for this is holy ground."

Moses fell to his knees, shielding his eyes with his hands. If it really was God speaking, he didn't want to look in his face. He would die of fright. Hurriedly, he took off his sandals to show respect.

"I have seen how my people suffer," said God. *"I have heard their cries and their prayers. I want you, Moses, to go back to Egypt and ask Pharaoh to let me take them out of Egypt. I shall lead them to a promised land; a place where they can live freely."*

Moses thought of Pharaoh sitting on his splendid throne, surrounded by his guards and ministers. This was the man whose forefather had ordered the killing of all Israelite boys. Surely such a king would not listen to a shepherd, a nomad, an Israelite?

"I will be with you," said God. *"Already I have asked your brother, Aaron, to come to meet you. He is a good speaker. You must tell the Israelites that I have heard their cry for help."*

"But will they believe me?" asked Moses. "What shall I tell them your name is?"

"I AM WHO I AM," thundered God. *"Say that I AM has sent you. That is my name: I AM. The Lord."*

The power of the voice made Moses huddle closer to the ground.

"Can you not send someone else to see Pharaoh?" he stammered. "I'm not very good at talking to kings, nor to anyone else for that matter. I… I have a stutter."

"Do not doubt me, I shall be with you all the way," promised God. *"I shall work miracles to convince the Egyptians*

that I mean to set my people free. Do not be afraid, Moses."

Moses picked himself up from the ground and stood tall. At last his life made sense. He realised that it was God who had saved his life on the Nile, who had led him out into the desert. God had done all this because he wanted Moses to lead the Israelites out of Egypt, to freedom. Moses knew he had an enormous task ahead of him, but he would do it and he would do it to God's satisfaction.

Calling his sheep, he climbed down Mount Horeb and returned to Jethro's camp. That same night, he gathered his family and set off back to Egypt – back to his people and his destiny.

The Passover

The Lord said to Moses, "Now you shall see what I will do to Pharaoh... by a mighty hand he will let them go; by a mighty hand he will drive them out of his land."

EXODUS 6:1

Egypt hadn't changed much in the years that Moses had been away. There was a new pharaoh on the throne but he was just as cruel, just as harsh on the Israelites, as his forefathers had been. Moses and his brother, Aaron, sought an audience with him. They were ushered into the enormous grand hall, fragrant with the smell of burning incense.

"The Lord, the God of Israel, requests that you let his people go that they might offer sacrifice up to him in the desert," said Aaron, speaking on behalf of his brother.

Pharaoh had been expecting two rich merchants bringing him gifts, not these two poor shepherds.

"I do not know your lord," he sneered. And he turned away, a sign that the audience was over. When Moses and Aaron left, Pharoah called a guard over.

"What cheek! How dare they ask me to release my slaves? Guard, make the Israelites work harder. Don't give them straw to make bricks with – command them to gather it themselves. But they must still produce the same number of bricks as before, or they will be punished."

When Moses and Aaron heard of this new decree, they requested a second audience. This time it was Moses who spoke.

"Let God's people go," he insisted.

"The Lord wills it. He commands it."

"I do not recognise your Israelite god," snapped Pharaoh. "Can he work miracles like my gods?"

Moses had been told by God that this challenge would come. He asked Aaron to throw his shepherd's crook to the ground. The stick instantly turned into a snake, hissing and writhing across the polished floor.

"Mere sleight of hand, Your Majesty," murmured one of the court magicians in Pharaoh's ear. The magician threw his wand to the ground. It too turned into a snake.

"There," laughed Pharaoh. "Apparently one of my court magicians is just as powerful as your god."

At the king's words, Aaron's snake leapt across the floor and, opening its mouth wide, swallowed the magician's snake whole. Pharaoh was taken aback for a moment.

"Take these men out," he ordered his guards, "and see to it that they do not come in again."

The guards showed Moses and Aaron out of the palace. But the next morning they were back again, waiting for Pharaoh near his barge on the bank of the river.

"You have refused to obey the Lord's command," shouted Moses, "so he is sending you another sign."

As Moses spoke, Aaron held his crook over the river. The Nile bubbled as if it were boiling and turned to blood. All over Egypt, people cried out. The water in the reservoirs, the lakes, even the palace ponds, had all turned to thick, putrid blood. The stench was unbearable.

Furious, Pharaoh returned to his palace. He summoned his magicians, asking them to repeat the trick.

"Your Majesty, we can turn soil to gold, create silver from river mud," said the magicians, "but we do not know how to turn water into blood. Give us time, Your Majesty, and we will discover the Israelite's secret."

Even as the magicians desperately consulted their books, the Nile turned to water once more. With relief, Pharaoh returned to his barge – only to find Moses and Aaron still there, waiting for him.

"Let God's people go," Aaron shouted across to the barge, "or there will be another punishment."

"I will not submit to any Israelite god, only an Egyptian one," snarled the king.

Aaron held out his stick again and this time thousands of frogs leapt out of the Nile. They hopped, croaking and squelching, across the muddy banks, through fields, streets and homes until they had overrun Egypt.

People found frogs everywhere – in their beds, in their cupboards, even in their ovens.

Now Pharaoh was feeling jittery. Bad news was coming in from across the land. The Egyptians were blaming him for this terrible curse that had been visited upon them. Pharaoh could not allow that – not when he was about to raise taxes again.

"Tell your god to take away these frogs," he told Moses and Aaron, "and I will let your people go."

The frogs died and their bodies were piled up in stinking heaps, ready for burning. Once more a powerful stench hung over Egypt. But now the plague was over, Pharaoh changed his mind.

"I need your people here," he said. "They have work to do, making bricks."

So Moses told Aaron to strike the ground with his crook. At once all the dust in Egypt turned into gnats. They swarmed everywhere, blotting out the sun, invading houses, shops and temples. They flew into people's eyes and hair, tormenting the elderly and making babies wail.

"Make these insects disappear!" Pharaoh screamed at his magicians. "I shall not be cowed by vermin."

But the sages only shook their heads, mystified, unable to come up with any explanation for the gnats.

"There is a god at work here much stronger than our own," they said. "Your Majesty, perhaps you should set the Israelites free?"

"That is for me to judge," shouted the king. "I am the one to decide if and when the people of Israel should be set free."

Outside, yet another plague was forming. Flies, millions of them, appeared out of thin air. They flew in great, buzzing clouds over houses, into palaces and temples, finding their way into every nook and cranny in the land. Only the region of Goshen, home of the Israelites, remained free of the plague.

The Lord wanted to show Pharaoh that he was the God of Israel.

At last, with his people angry and his land blighted, the vain king relented.

"Take your people," Pharaoh ordered Moses. "Let them go into the desert and worship your god."

dead in their runs. Only in Goshen were the animals spared.

This made Pharaoh even more angry. Who was this unknown god, this foreign deity, who would destroy all his animals at will? Was he more powerful than Seth, stronger than Osiris? No, he was not.

But hardly had Moses and Aaron left the king's presence than yet again he changed his mind.

"Why should I lose all my slaves?" he thought. "Egypt cannot survive without their labour. I will keep them, for the sake of my gods and their temples."

This time God's fury erupted on to the animals owned by the Egyptians. In fields, in meadows, in pens made of stone and wood, cattle keeled over and died. There were dead animals all over Egypt; cows and horses, donkeys and goats, even geese and hens were found

Pharoah knew the gods of Egypt were the most powerful, the greatest. He would show the Israelites whose wishes mattered in his land…

The king had still not learnt his lesson. As he ranted in his court, Moses held up a handful of ashes. The wind carried them out of his hand, turning them into a vast and deadly whirlwind. Everywhere they flew, people broke out in boils. Their faces, their hands, their backs were all covered with sores. Not even the nobles in the

palace were spared. The king, fearing he too might be affected, screamed for his magicians. But they had no cure for the boils, no antidote, no remedy. They were covered in boils themselves.

Moses was sure that the king would relent now. Who could not be affected by the sounds of children wailing in fear and pain? Who would let the elderly and the weak suffer for his vanity?

But Pharaoh remained stubborn. He defied the Lord's will. God sent more punishments: hailstorms destroyed every tree in Egypt; waves of locusts ate the harvest, leaving the fields bare; darkness covered the land for three whole days.

Yet despite the suffering, the deaths, the sadness of his people, Pharaoh still refused to let the Israelites go free.

"*I will visit one more punishment on the Egyptians,*" God said to Moses, "*and this time you will be set free. Now, let the people of Israel do as I command: On the tenth day of this month, every Israelite household will roast a lamb or a young goat. It has to be male and healthy. The people must smear some of the lamb or goat's blood on the doorpost, to show that Israelites live in the house. Then, dressed in their travelling clothes, with their belongings in bundles ready for the journey, they must eat the lamb.*"

Moses carried the word of God to the Israelites and they obeyed, daubing their doors with blood and then sitting down to eat their final meal, with their possessions in bundles around them. That night, the Angel of Death passed over the land, its face hidden in a veil of thick cloud. In every house the angel passed, the first-born son

crushed. What had he done? His vanity, his stubbornness, had caused the death of his dearest child – of so many innocent children.

"Let the Israelites go," whispered Pharaoh to his general, "and tell them to take their god with them. Give them gold for their journey, too, and all the jewellery you can find.

died quietly in his dreams. Only sons in the houses that were daubed with blood were spared – the children of the Israelites.

At dawn, Pharaoh woke up to heart-breaking news. His son, the heir to the Egyptian throne, was dead in his cot, his little body blue and cold. Pharaoh stood motionless by the infant's cradle,

I want you to make sure they won't ever, ever come back."

All over Goshen doors flew open, sandals were donned and bundles hoisted onto backs.

At last the people of Israel were free to go! They were leaving Egypt, leaving slavery. They were going to the land of their fathers – the Promised Land.

The Parting of the Red Sea

"Do not be afraid, stand firm...
the Egyptians whom you see today you shall never see again.
The Lord will fight for you and you have only to keep still."

EXODUS 14:13–14

Several days after the Israelites had left Egypt a messenger ran in to Pharaoh's palace.

"Your Majesty, work on your new temple has had to stop. The builders have run out of bricks."

"Go back and tell them to get the Israelites to make some more..."

"But, Your Majesty..."

Pharoah raised himself off his throne. The Israelites were gone. Egypt had lost one of its biggest assets and he,

the king, had allowed it to happen.

A general leant towards him and whispered, "They can't have gone very far, Your Majesty. Remember, they are weighed down with goods and children. It won't be difficult to catch up with them and force them to come back."

"Yes!" Pharoah nodded. What a fool he'd been to give in to Moses and his invisible god! True, he'd lost his eldest son, but surely that had just been a tragedy, a whim of nature, not a punishment from a god?

"Prepare my chariots," he said. "We are going to bring those Israelites back."

Tents were put up, fires lit, water boiled. Bread was baked on hot stones – a flat, hard bread that cooked quickly. Then some children, fetching water from the lake, heard the thundering of hooves. A plume of smoke seemed to spread across the horizon. It was sand, kicked up by horses and chariots.

"The Egyptians are coming!"

The cry went up all over the camp. "It's an attack!
We're going to die."

On the banks of the Red Sea – marshy ground that was often flooded – the Israelites had set up camp. The Lord, hidden in a pillar of cloud by day and in a pillar of fire by night, had led them here to rest, to regain their strength before beginning their journey towards the Promised Land.

Men and women looked up, their hands frozen, the food halfway to their mouths. The Israelites were trapped between the sea in front and the Egyptian army behind. Panic spread through the crowds like fire through dry brushwood.

"Moses, what are we going to do?

Aaron, where is your god when we need him?"

Moses ignored the jibes, the doubts. God was talking in his ear, telling him what to do.

"*Hold your crook out over the water; you will never be bothered by the Egyptians again.*"

Moses held up his shepherd's crook. A wind, hot and strong, started blowing from the east. The water moved, piling up in two enormous waves, clearing a muddy path in between. The pillar of cloud, hiding God, moved onto the path.

"Come on, God wants us to follow him."

The Israelites picked up their belongings and followed Moses and Aaron as they walked out across the seabed. On either side of them the water stood as solid as stone, two long walls of sparkling azure.

"Look, there's a fish, swimming high up in the water."

"There's an octopus!"

"A dolphin!"

"Hush now, children," their mother said. "We must hurry."

On they went, the mud squelching over their sandals, the seabed icy cold under their hot, tired feet.

Far behind them, Pharaoh saw the crowds of Israelites disappear as if by magic.

"Where have they gone?"

Riding a chariot close to Pharaoh's, an Egyptian general shook his head.

"They have dived into the sea. Seeing us must have driven them mad with fear."

One of the court magicians riding with Pharaoh gasped, "They are not drowned. Look – the sea has parted to let them through!"

The Pharaoh gaped in astonishment. Then his amazement turned to anger.

Who was this strange god who could work such miracles, who dared to mock the greatest king on Earth? Pharaoh would show this god that his power knew no bounds either. He would pursue the Israelites and bring them back to Egypt in chains.

reached dry land on the other side. People and animals scrambled to safety, pulling their belongings behind them. Soon the last few people were climbing over the wet rocks onto dry sand.

Not far behind, the great king paused in the middle of the sea, his golden

"Follow me!" he cried to his men.

Recklessly, Pharaoh's chariot plunged into the muddy chasm, its wheels skidding on seaweed. The army followed, horses rearing in fear, the soldiers fitting arrows to their bows.

Ahead of them, the Israelites' pace quickened. The front of the crowd had

chariot splattered with mud. His eyes were fixed on Moses, shepherding the last of the crowd up the bank to safety. Pharaoh raised his spear, ready to hurl it at his old enemy.

Just then, a groaning rumble passed through the walls of water on either side of the Egyptians. Silver fish turned, scattered and bolted. Pharaoh only had time to turn and glare at his general before the water came crashing down on him, filling the chasm. Horses and chariots, generals, soldiers and archers were swept off their feet, smashed against each other and dashed on the spiky rocks. In the space of a single moment, not one of them was left alive. They were all drowned, the might of Egypt lost in an instant.

On the shore of the Red Sea, the Israelites stood in silence, thunderstruck by this example of God's power. The Egyptians, their captors, their masters, who had enslaved them for hundreds of years, were gone at last, out of their lives forever.

Miriam, Moses's sister, picked up a tambourine and started singing:

"I will sing to the Lord, for He has Triumphed gloriously.
The horse and his rider
He has thrown into the sea."

Other women took up her song, their voices uniting in the chill desert air. In the distance, beyond the sea, the sun set over Egypt, leaving behind the darkness of night.

At last the Israelite people were free.

The Ten Commandments

When God finished speaking with Moses on Mount Sinai,
he gave him the two tablets of the covenant,
tablets of stone, written with the finger of God.

EXODUS 31:18

For three long months, the people of Israel followed the pillar of cloud and fire. Deeper and deeper into the desert they went, until the pillar came to rest beside a mountain called Mount Sinai. The people looked up at the steep rocks towering above them. They were smooth as copper. Not a blade of grass, not a tuft of soft moss could be seen growing anywhere.

"Moses, why did we stop here? Surely you're not asking us to climb over that mountain? Think of the old people, the children…"

"We are here for a reason," said Moses, "a very important reason. Set up camp. I will have soon have more instructions for you."

With that, he picked up his staff and a flask of water and started climbing up the rocks, picking his way carefully over the dusty boulders. The people watched him in amazement. Where was Moses going?

But there was no time to stand about and wonder. The sun was getting hot and the people had work to do. The men unfurled their tents; the women beat the fleas out of the bedding so that the children could have an afternoon nap. By the time they had finished lighting the fires and setting the cooking pots over them, Moses had come back down the mountain again.

"Call the elders of the tribes," he said. "Let them gather round – I have great news."

The elders came, their robes pulled tight around them against the cold desert air of the evening.

"God has spoken to me," Moses told them. "He wants to make an agreement with us, a covenant. He has chosen us to be his special people, but only if we agree to live by his rules."

"What are his rules?" asked some of the men.

"What kind of agreement?" others wanted to know.

"Hush," said the elders. "We will do whatever God asks of us."

Moses carried the people's words back up the mountain to God.

"They accept," he said. "The people of Israel will do your bidding."

"*Then go and tell them that I shall come to speak to them,*" answered God. "*In three days' time I shall come down from the mountain, so that they might see my power.*"

Moses hurried back to the camp. The people trembled with fear when they heard the news. God – coming to speak to them? How could they face him, they who had mistrusted and doubted his word? What if he saw straight into their hearts and knew which of them had complained about the scarcity of food, the hard journey or the lack of water?

"Do not worry," said Moses. "God is kind, he knows we are weak. But let's get to work. We must prepare ourselves for his coming."

Everyone set about tidying up the camp. Tents were swept clean, mattresses aired, dirty clothes washed and cooking pots scoured and left out in the sun to dry. Mothers bathed their children and soaped them until their skin smelt like flowers in a temple.

Three days later, the people of Israel woke up to grey skies. There was a strange smell of burning in the air, as if a great storm was about to unleash itself on the desert. From high up on Mount Sinai came the distant rumble of thunder. A thick cloud, black as soot, was advancing slowly down the mountain, swallowing everything in its path: rocks, boulders and stunted trees with leafless branches. Little mountain birds, no larger than bats, were swooping away from the cloud in a blind panic.

In the camp below, the people waited in silence. Children tightened their grip on their parents' hands. Lambs bleated, hiding behind their mothers. Suddenly there was a flash of lightning that seemed to hit the very top of Mount Sinai. The mountain started to shake

and a flock of desert vultures took to the air shrieking their alarm across the sky.

The sound of a deafening trumpet echoed around the dusty hills.

"Come," Moses called to the frightened people. "Do not be afraid. God is calling us."

Slowly, moving as one, the people of Israel came out of their camp. Fear made their hearts beat fast in their chests. Their feet felt like lead. At the top of the mountain, a huge ball of flame was showing through the thick cloud. It was God, shielded by fire from the eyes of the people. The trumpet blew on and on, until it seemed that its blare was making the sky itself tremble.

Some people, those closest to the copper-brown rocks, could see Moses walking up the lower slopes of the mountain. His lips were moving, his eyes fixed on the distant fire at the summit. His brother Aaron joined him and together they picked their way through the boulders until they were lost to the people watching below, lost in the billows of dark cloud.

At the summit, God was waiting for them, hidden in his camouflage of fire and flame.

His voice, coming from the flame, sounded like the roar of thunder.

"These are my Ten Commandments:

I am your God. Worship no one but me.
Do not make idols or pray to false gods.
Treat my name with respect.
Do not work on the sabbath, the seventh
day of the week, keep it to honour me.
Respect your father and your mother.
Do not kill other people.

Husbands and wives, you must be faithful
to each other.
Do not steal.
Do not tell lies.
Do not long for other people's belongings.
Obey these commandments and you shall
be my own special people."

Moses went down to the foot of the mountain and called out these laws to the Israelites.

"We shall obey God's laws," promised the people when Moses had finished speaking. "We shall keep our covenant with the Lord."

To show God that the people had accepted his laws, Moses directed his men to build an altar at the foot of the mountain, with six pillars on each side – one for every tribe of Israel. Then they offered sacrifice on it; a healthy ox from one of their herds.

When the sacrifice was over, Moses told them, "People of Israel, I need to go up the mountain one last time. I may be gone for quite a while, so I am leaving Aaron in charge. Obey him as you would me."

Moses set off once more towards the summit of Mount Sinai. This time he stayed up there for forty days and forty nights, hidden from the people of Israel far below, listening as God explained how he expected his chosen people to live.

God told Moses that he expected everyone to treat each other with respect and honesty. He wanted people to trust and love one another. When someone sinned, they were to offer a sacrifice to show that they had truly repented.

God wanted his people to have festivals – days of joy and prayer. There were to be three festivals: the first, Passover, to celebrate their escape from Egypt, would be marked by the eating of unleavened bread, like the bread they had made for their journey. The second would be a celebration of the first fruits of the season; the third would be to thank God for the gift of each year's harvest.

God gave Moses instructions to build an ark. This time the ark was to be a sacred chest, carried on poles, in which the people of Israel were to keep the laws God had given them and through which God would speak to his chosen people.

Surrounding the ark was to be the tabernacle – a magnificent tent of finely-woven cloth that the Israelites could take with them and use for meetings and for worship during their long journey across the desert to the Promised Land.

When, at last, God had finished speaking, He handed Moses two stone tablets. On them, back and front, were carved the Ten Commandments, written in God's own hand.

"Take them to the people," God commanded, *"so that they will never forget my instructions."*

Moses, his face shining with the light of God, set off down the mountain to deliver the sacred tablets to the people.

The Ark of the Covenant

The Lord said to Moses . . . "Go up to a land flowing with milk and honey; but I will not go up among you, or I would consume you on the way, for you are a stiff-necked people."

EXODUS 33:1, 3

Down on the plain, the people kept glancing up at the mountain. Moses had been away for over a month. Each time they looked, they saw only dark clouds, blown about by the wind.

"Moses has been gone a long time, Aaron," grumbled the Israelites, their faces darkened and lips chapped by the fierce sun. "Are you sure he is still alive? Can an old man survive that long on a mountain, without food or shelter?"

Aaron shut himself away in his tent. He needed to think. What if Moses really was dead? Who would lead the people then? How would they find their way to the Promised Land?

"Aaron, the people are afraid. We need a god to pray to, a god we can see – not one who lives on top of a mountain, hidden behind a curtain of clouds."

A crowd was gathering outside the tent. Their footsteps and anxious voices grew closer. They had chosen young men to speak for them, to voice their fears and desires:

"Aaron, we need a god that will lead us out of this desert."

"One we can see."

"One we can deck with flowers and sing to."

The people were insistent. They needed a god they could see and touch, a god like the ones they had become used to in Egypt – a fearsome god with the head of a raven, perhaps, or a crocodile.

"Gather your gold and your jewellery," said Aaron, striding out of the tent. He couldn't resist the will of the people any longer. "You shall have your idol to worship."

With whoops of joy, the people gathered their precious trinkets: bracelets and coins and earrings shaped like rising suns. In huge wicker baskets the booty was taken to Aaron. A mould was carved in the shape of a fat calf, with an open mouth to show glinting teeth and pointed horns on its head. The people's gold was melted in big vats, poured into the mould and allowed to set. Soon the

huge golden calf stood glittering on its plinth, its horns pointing defiantly at the blazing sky, with an altar standing before it.

Someone started playing a harp, another fetched a drum. Soon people were singing, dancing and swaying together in large circles around the golden idol.

As he hurried down the mountain-side with the stone tablets, Moses heard music – the kind played in Egyptian temples. In the fading sunlight, he caught sight of glimmering gold and smelt the burning of a sacrifice. Aaron saw his brother coming slowly down the mountain path and went to meet him. "What are the people doing?" asked Moses.

"They thought you were dead. They believed God had abandoned them, so they made another one, a golden calf."

"Another god, a false god."

So much for the chosen peoples' promise to their God. So much for the first commandment, broken within a few short weeks. In anger, Moses raised the tablets high above his head and smashed them on the ground. The tablets shattered into a thousand pieces, bouncing away down the mountain.

The people, hearing a wild howl of rage, looked up from the golden calf. The dancers stopped, their faces shining with sweat. The musicians hid their tambourines behind their backs, like children caught stealing fruit at a market stall. Moses advanced towards them. His face had been shining with joy, as he picked his way down the mountain. Now his eyes were brimming with anger and disbelief.

"Melt that thing down! It must be destroyed. This is a terrible sin in the eyes of the Lord. Will he forgive us? Or will he cast us out, like lepers from the city?"

At once, hammers were fetched and the golden calf was smashed to bits. The gold was melted, the altar standing before it dismantled.

A few days passed before Moses returned once more to the top of Mount Sinai, to speak with God. Here he pleaded on behalf of his foolish people for God to forgive their sin.

Moses appealed to God, saying that people could be feeble, especially when faced with doubt, fear and sadness. He asked God to punish him, for the sins of the Children of Israel. Eventually God forgave his chosen people.

"Carve me two new tablets," he said to Moses, *"and I will inscribe the Ten Commandments again. Then you must build the sacred Tent of Meeting – I am coming with you on your journey to the Promised Land."*

Thankful for God's mercy, the people set about preparing his sacred tent. They brought wood and cloth and thread. Many offered spices, oils and fragrant incense to burn and jewels to display. So many gifts were brought, so much gold and precious metal laid at the smelters' feet, that Moses had to turn whole crowds away.

Two gifted craftsmen, Bezalel and Oholiab, were chosen to organise the work, to draw God's designs and to make sure everything was constructed to the highest standard. The best carvers, the most talented joiners, sculptors and weavers offered their services. Day and night they worked, sawing, hammering, sculpting, weaving and sewing.

The weavers and seamstresses, their fingers nimble from years of service in

Egypt, made curtains out of linen. The woodworkers carved poles for the frame from precious acacia wood; the blacksmiths cast bronze and golden hooks. Before long the sacred tent stood in the desert, its linen curtains decorated with beautiful winged creatures, its roof padded with goats hair to keep out dew and rain. Following God's instructions, Bezalel divided the tent into two rooms. The first was for the priests, to offer sacrifice and pray to God on behalf of the people. A golden altar, a lamp stand, a table laden with precious bowls and cups were placed in it, hidden from the crowds by costly curtains. The second room was for God himself, the Holy of Holies. No one would be allowed to part its curtains, to tread inside it. No one except the high priest, the holy leader of the people who had yet to be chosen. He would come in once a year, on a day of festival, to ask God's forgiveness for the people's sins.

Another curtain, a wall of rich, embroidered linen, was put up around

the tent. Bezalel and Oholiab then made a chest, the ark of the covenant, using acacia wood. On its lid they placed two carved angels covered in gold. The angels faced one another with their wings spread out to form a space where God could rest, hidden from the people.

As instructed by God, Moses put the new tablets with God's writing on them inside the ark. Its lid sealed, it was placed in God's chamber, the Holy of Holies. The sacred tent was ready at last and it was magnificent.

Moses fetched his brother Aaron, and Aaron's sons, and gave them fine robes to wear, decorated with jewels.

"You are the high priest of God," he said to Aaron, "and your sons are the priests. You will be in charge of the temple and all that goes on within it."

A ceremony was held – a sacrifice of a bull and a lamb was offered and the tent was blessed with oil to make it fit for God. As the people prayed, a great cloud descended on the temple and God's light filled every corner and crease of its costly curtains. The people trembled; they knew God had arrived.

When at last the cloud lifted and the light dispersed, the people dismantled the tent and packed it away on donkeys and camels. Poles covered with gold were put through the rings of the ark, so that the priests could carry it without touching the holy vessel. Then Moses gave the word and, weighed down with all their belongings, their animals and the new tent, the Children of Israel left Mount Sinai forever.

As the mountain grew smaller and smaller in the distance, they did not look back to whisper quick prayers. God was not hidden by thick cloud on the mountain any more. He was travelling with his people – wherever they went he was with them.

The Promised Land

"Not one of these — not one of this evil generation — shall see the good land that I swore to give to your ancestors, except Caleb . . . because of his complete fidelity."

DEUTERONOMY 1:35–36

The Children of Israel had left the desert of Sinai and were wending their way northward across the tough, scorching wilderness where only lizards and snakes survived. God helped them on their journey – manna would appear as if from the sky and quail, tame and ready for the pot, arrived on the wind. Then at long last they reached the edge of the desert. Shimmering in the hazy distance stood Canaan, a vast country, green, hilly and shrouded in mist.

God spoke from the light of the tent of meeting, his voice carrying on the evening breeze.

"Behold the land I have given you. The Promised Land."

There it was – the reward for their faith in God, shaky as it was, the glittering prize of the covenant.

But what kind of country was this Promised Land, wondered the elders. Was it rich and fertile? Would it be large enough for all of them? Who rules it now? Was it owned by nomads, cruel warriors or rich kings who would send powerful armies to crush them and force them back into slavery?

Moses and Aaron chose twelve men as spies to enter Canaan and come back with information. The men left like wolves in the night, silent, quick, mingling with the local people as they approached the border. When they came back, forty days later, they had all sorts of news, and information for the elders.

"Canaan is rich and fertile – an amazing land." said Joshua, speaking to the people first. "Look, we brought pomegranates, figs and huge bunches of sweet grapes."

Caleb, his friend, was just as eager.

"There are big, rich cities, surrounded by thick walls. But we can easily overpower them."

The other spies frowned, they had not been so impressed.

"Yes, but the people are giants and their soldiers ride swift chariots and throw spears."

"Giants?" the people in the crowd murmured. "Has God brought us all this way to be crushed like grasshoppers under the feet of giants?"

"Don't lose courage," said Joshua, "God is on our side. He will help us."

"And there are lots of poor people too," added Caleb, "fed up with their rich kings and masters, just as we were tired of the Egyptians. I'm sure they would join in the fight to overcome the kings. They would be our allies."

It seemed as if the desert sun had addled the people's minds. They would

not listen to Joshua and Caleb, only to the spies who told them dreadful news.

"Why, oh why, did God drag us all the way here, to a foreign land filled with killers and giants? Someone lead us back to Egypt – we might be slaves there, but we'll be safe from harm and we'll have plenty to eat."

Back to Egypt! Back to slavery and false gods? God heard the people's grumbling and he was angry. Had he not parted the Red Sea for them? Had he not provided food and water? How could they doubt his intentions again?

"*You are ungrateful people,*" he thundered that night, his light blazing from the Tent of Meeting. "*I work miracles for you and yet you still question my plans.*"

"Forgive them, Lord," begged Moses, shouting through the embroidered curtain, his face close to the ground.

But this time the Lord would not forgive the people. They had sinned against him one time too many.

"*None of you who left Egypt will enter the Promised Land. None except Joshua and Caleb, who brought good news, will taste the fruit of its vineyards. The rest of you will die out here in the wilderness; your bones will be bleached by the sun, your names forgotten. Go, depart from me – you shall live in the desert for forty years, one for every day the spies spent in the Promised Land.*"

The light dimmed they were left in darkness.

"*I, the Lord, have spoken.*"

When the people heard God's pronouncement, they changed their minds about going back to Egypt. What – head back to slavery and to making mudbricks all day long? No. They hadn't crossed plain and desert, suffered thirst and disease, only to return back to drudgery. They'd been promised a land of their own, and they were going to have it.

The very next day, a band of men tried to attack Canaan to gain a foothold in the hills, but they were beaten back and returned wounded, defeated and disheartened. God was sticking to His word – the Israelites were forced to wander around the desert, trying to find a way into the Promised Land but kept away by the enemy. The people complained again and again.

"We have no shelter, Moses."

"Aaron, there are no grapes, no figs – there is no grain left in our stores – we don't even have water!"

At last, in the bleak wilderness of Zin, the muttering and grumbling became deafening.

"*I will give the people water,*" God said, speaking to Moses and Aaron. "*Go to that rock over there and order the water to flow out of it, in my name.*"

Moses and Aaron gathered the people.

"You shall have water," said Moses, "and plenty of it. Here it is."

And he struck the rock twice with his stick. But Moses did not say that it was God making the water flow, quenching the people's thirst. The water appeared just the same, gushing out of the sun-warmed stone in huge, foaming torrents. The people drank and watered their animals; and then filled their jars and goatskins for later. Moses enjoyed the people's thanks, basking in the warmth of their praise.

"You have sinned against me, Moses and Aaron," said God. "I told you to order the water to come forth in my name, not to hit the rock with your stick, as if it was YOU who were working a miracle."

Moses and Aaron fell to their knees, asking the Lord's forgiveness, but God spoke harshly and decisively.

"Because you did not honour me, you will not enter the Promised Land."

Soon afterwards Aaron died; his robes and his role as priest passed on to his son. Moses lived on for many years, leading his people in the wilderness, making sure they kept their bargain with God. As the forty years of punishment drew to a close, Moses chose Joshua as his successor, blessing him and ordering the people to obey Joshua's word as they had obeyed his own. Moses then climbed to the top of a mountain, old, his skin burnt and wrinkled by the sun, but as strong as ever, his eyes still bright. Light filled the sky as he reached the summit and he could see right across the River Jordan, into the Promised Land – across its vineyards and valleys, its hills and crags, its towns and cities.

"*Behold, Moses, the Promised Land. The country I promised Abraham and Isaac and Jacob.*"

"It's a fine country for your chosen people, Lord. Thank you."

The sun set, a chill swept across the mountain and Moses, the great leader, closed his eyes for the last time. His work was done, his journey over. God himself buried Moses in the desert, in a spot where no one would ever find his bones.

Moses was gone. At the foot of the mountain, the people of Israel turned to Joshua. This strong and courageous warrior was their leader now. He would lead God's people and they would obey his every word.

The forty years of punishment were over. The people who had left Egypt, their few belongings strapped to their backs, had all passed away. In their place stood their children; raised in the desert, hammered into shape by the heat and the sun, ready to do God's will.

It was time to conquer the Promised Land.

Rahab and the Spies

"I know that the Lord has given you the land, and that dread of you has fallen on us . . . The Lord your God is indeed God in heaven above and on earth below."

JOSHUA 2:9, 11

Joshua stood on the banks of the River Jordan and pointed across the rushing water to the distant walls of a fortified city.

"Up ahead lies the first city of the Promised Land we are going to conquer. The city of palm trees – Jericho."

The young men around him gazed at the city with fire in their eyes. The walls were high and thick and there were houses built into them. Guards marched along the ramparts, spears above their shoulders – word had reached them that the Israelites were coming, that they wanted to take the city, and the place was on high alert.

"I want two of you to act as spies," said Joshua. "Find out what you can about the king and his army. Do they know we are coming? When do they expect us to attack? Are they waiting for help from other kings?"

The two men chosen for job were good hunters, natural spies. They'd learnt the art of moving unnoticed and reading hidden meanings behind every noise they heard, every movement they saw. That night, when the moon was hidden by clouds, they swam across the river. The rising sun dried their clothes but they waited until it was nearly noon to come out from hiding. In the glare of the midday sun, they slipped out and mingled with the crowds going in and out of the city. They'd chosen a market day for the trip, so the streets were busy, the din of the hawkers deafening.

"Who'd like fresh meat? Sweet water? Ripe dates?"

They walked through the open gates, noticing how thick they were, how heavily guarded.

The streets of Jericho were straight but narrow, beautifully paved but rank with the smell of rotting vegetables. There were houses on either side them, all with flat roofs, some with outdoor ovens belching smoke. A Canaanite temple rose high above the rooftops to their left. As they stood in the street, taking note, the crowds thinned. People were going home for their midday rest, to escape the heat of the early afternoon.

"We should have something to eat too," said one of the spies.

It was agreed – they should get off the street before they attracted too much attention. Now that the streets were emptying, people were starting to look at them suspiciously.

Perhaps they were intrigued by the dried mud on their feet, or maybe it was the strange cut of their clothes.

"There's an inn there – look – right by the city gate. Let's see if we can get a meal."

They ducked into the gloom of the crowded inn. There were a lot of men about, eating, drinking, swearing loudly. A woman approached them.

"I am Rahab – I own this house. Would you like some wine and perhaps some pleasant company?'

"Some wine would be good. And two bowls of stew, if you have any."

"I have stew. Come, there is a room upstairs, where the air is fresher."

Rahab's pretty earrings jangled as she led the way up narrow stairs to a chamber with cushions on the floor.

"You are Hebrews, are you not?" she said, turning to the two men, her voice just a whisper. "Don't be afraid, I will not give you away."

The two spies obviously did not believe her. They looked around them, searching for a way to escape.

"You have already been recognised," whispered Rahab. "Everyone is under strict orders from the king to report any strangers seen in the city. You'd better hide somewhere, the guards will be here before you know it."

Even as she spoke, they could hear a loud murmur in the street outside.

Rahab led them out onto a flat roof, partly shaded by a gnarled vine. On the roof were great mounds of flax, drying in the sun.

The two men had just wriggled under the drying stalks when someone started pounding on Rahab's door.

"King's orders. Let us in."

She leaned coolly over the balustrade, flashing her famous smile at the angry faces below.

"My guests are sleeping off their meal, gentlemen. Please do not disturb them."

"You have Israelites in your house. They were seen entering the inn."

"There were two Israelites here, but they left. They heard we close the city gates before dusk and they were eager to get out. My girls tried to keep them here with sweet words but they would have none of it. You know what the Hebrews are like – they don't much care for such pleasures."

"Oh! We've missed our chance."

The disappointment in the captain's voice told Rahab she had won. She was a popular citizen with powerful friends, and men had a foolish tendency to believe her every word. Today they had no choice really. Even if they thought she was harbouring enemies, they would have to get special permission to enter her house – in Jericho it was forbidden for men to enter a free woman's home without her consent. The guards left, marching down the street in their heavy sandals, but they stationed two men by her door, in case the spies returned.

Rahab returned to the mounds of flax on her roof. She couldn't send the two men out on to the street, but she could show them another way to escape. Her house was built into the city walls – the spies could climb out of an outside window, shin down a rope, and they'd be out of Jericho.

As she watched the Israelites dust bits of flax from their hair, she wondered what had made her help them. They were the enemy. Everyone in the city was terrified of the Israelites. They had been wandering around Canaan for years, waiting to invade. She should be giving them up to the king, not helping them to escape.

"They say you worship a powerful god who wins victories for you," she said to the spies. "There's even a story about how he made the sea swallow an Egyptian pharaoh and his men. If your army takes this city, perhaps you will remember my kindness?"

One of the spies undid a red cord from around his waist.

"Hang this from your window, and our men will spare you and everyone under your roof. We promise, for you have done the Lord's work today."

Later she would do as they asked, but for now she tied the cord around her head, then showed the men to the window. It was small and high up in the wall but they climbed through it easily, like foxes escaping from a grain store.

The last she saw of them, the Israelites were heading off to the hills in the late afternoon haze, as soldiers searched the glimmering banks of the River Jordan.

The Walls of Jericho

"You shall not shout or let your voice be heard,
nor shall you utter a word, until the day
I tell you to shout. Then you shall shout."

JOSHUA 6:10

The two spies returned to the Israelites, camped across the river from Jericho. Joshua listened carefully to everything the spies had to say.

"The city is well fortified," reported the first spy, "but the Canaanites are scared of us. They know we are planning to take Jericho. The soldiers are disheartened."

"We had a good look at the city walls too," added the second. "Strong and well-built – but there are one or two places where we can scale them. There are even dwellings built into the walls."

Joshua discussed the information with his other leaders, all courageous men who had with their own ideas on how they could invade Jericho.

"We could scale the walls."

"We could smash the city gate. All it would take is a dozen men. The archers could follow them."

"The most pressing problem is how to get our people across the Jordan. Its banks are flooding at this time of year. The water flows swiftly, dangerously…"

In the night, God spoke to Joshua, his voice carried on the wind.

"Tomorrow, tell the priests to carry the ark of the covenant into the waters of the Jordan."

The priests did as Joshua told them. The moment their feet touched the cold water, there was a booming crash further upstream. The banks of the river had collapsed into it. Water started to pile up against the new dam, swirling angrily, rising in mud-brown eddies.

Downstream the river continued to flow, past Jericho to the salt sea of Arabah. The water level started to fall and before long the riverbed showed through, the wet pebbles winking like jewels in the fierce sun. Not since God helped them to cross the Red Sea, had water parted like this. The priests

carrying the ark walked to the middle of the riverbed and the Israelites, knowing what God wanted from them, crossed the river. When the last person reached the other side, the priests carried the ark across. As soon as they were safely on the other side, the dam upstream broke with a crash and nut-brown water rushed downriver again, flooding the Israelites' path once more and then overflowing the banks of the Jordan.

When news of this arrived in Jericho, the Canaanites were dumbstruck with awe and fear. They had heard rumours about the Israelites and their strange god who handed them victories on golden platters. Now the rumours had come true – here was their army, safely across the water, ready to attack them!

What would these Israelites do first? Try to scale the city walls? Attempt to smash in the city gates with a battering ram? Starve out the people? It was harvest time so most of the food supplies hadn't been brought into the city yet – Jericho was at its most vulnerable.

But nothing happened. No trees were felled to make a battering ram. No ladders were constructed to scale the city walls. God had other plans for how his people would take their first city in the Promised Land – mysterious, spectacular plans. This battle would be remembered for the rest of time. He gave Joshua precise instructions.

The next morning, Joshua gathered the Israelite army with all its weapons. They led seven priests, each one blowing a large trumpet made from a ram's horn, around the city of Jericho. Behind the seven priests came others, carrying the ark of the covenant on poles. The rest of the people brought up the rear,

walking in silence. Only the sound of the horns echoed across the plain and through the city.

The people of Jericho gathered on the walls, everyone pushing to get a better view, everyone voicing an opinion. Would the Israelites attack after the march? Would they scale the walls and burn down the gates? No – the priests led the people around the city once and then back to their new camp on the riverbank. There the Israelites lit fires for cooking and began repairing their weapons. The Canaanites found it all very strange and unsettling.

The same thing happened for the next five days. Every morning the Israelites followed their priests round the city in complete silence, listening to the eerie sound of those blaring trumpets. On the seventh day, though, the march did not stop after the first circuit. The Israelites kept on walking, circle after circle, until they had gone round Jericho seven times. Then Joshua lifted his arms and his people started shouting and cheering, clapping and stamping their feet. The walls of the city shook with the sound of the Israelites. The soldiers and onlookers standing on the walls, the market traders in the streets, the people in their houses, all felt the ground tremble beneath their feet. Animals whined and howled, birds screeched and took flight as temples started to sway, houses to tumble and bridges to collapse. The walls crumbled, stone by stone, falling into the great valley below. God had shaken the earth itself to give Jericho to the Israelites.

The soldiers, those that survived, picked up arms. But there was no one to bark orders, no one to lead them. The Israelites were everywhere, clambering over the ruins, swarming along the streets. Their eyes were filled with the courage of their God, the conviction of their beliefs. The gods of Jericho, of Canaan, on the other hand, seemed to have deserted their people. Their temples had been toppled, destroyed.

As God had instructed them, the Israelites spared no one in Jericho – not farmer, freeman, soldier or slave. Only in one house did thankful voices rise to greet a new day. It was built into the city walls and from one of its windows a red cord fluttered in the morning breeze…

Samson and Delilah

*"Coax him, and find out what makes his strength so great . . .
so that we may bind him in order to subdue him; and we
will each give you eleven hundred pieces of silver."*

JUDGES 16:5

Little by little, the Israelites conquered Canaan, the Promised Land. They did not manage to drive out all the Canaanites, so they had to share the land with them. In time, Joshua died and the Israelites forgot their promise to God. They were lured into worshipping the false gods of Canaan and burning sacrifices on their altars.

God was angry and helped the Canaanites to rise up against the Israelites. Tribe after tribe attacked them until one group, the Philistines, conquered God's people. The Israelites prayed for their deliverance, but it was useless; he seemed to ignore their prayers and sacrifices.

One day, nearly forty years after the Philistines had conquered the Israelites, a man called Manoah and his wife were in the fields near their home in Zorah, when a stranger approached.

"Manoah, you shall have a son."

"I am old," answered Manoah, "and my wife is past the age when she can bear children. Do not insult me."

"Nevertheless, she is going to have a son and that man will help free the Israelites from the Philistines. Bring him up as a holy man, for I have great plans for him. He must never touch anything that is dead. Nor must he have wine or strong drink. Most of all, he must not cut his hair. If he keeps his hair long, as a sign of respect to me, he will be stronger than any man or beast that roams the earth."

The messenger smiled, held up his hands, and was gone. Manoah realised he had been talking to an angel – a messenger from God. When the child was born, his parents called him Samson and he grew up to be as strong as the angel of God had foretold.

Samson loved God, but he did not listen to his parents' warning about what God wanted from him. He broke God's commandments, he drank wine, and he touched the bodies of animals he hunted. But his favourite pastime was taunting the Philistines, burning their crops and pulling down their city gates with his bare hands.

One afternoon, he was drinking from a well when a shadow fell across his cupped hands. Samson looked up to see a woman standing in front of him. He could tell by her dress that she was a Philistine, his enemy, but he firmly pushed that thought out of his head. Samson loved the company of women, and Delilah was the most beautiful woman he had ever seen.

Delilah invited Samson to supper at her house and he followed her meekly, like a puppy following its master. At the end of the evening, he begged her to invite him again. Soon Samson was hopelessly in love with the Philistine. Little did he suspect that her kisses were not loaded with love, but with greed and treachery. The Philistine leaders had promised her a large fortune if she could find out what made Samson strong. They wanted to get rid of Canaan's strongest enemy and show that the Israelite God was weak.

Night after night, Delilah plied Samson with fine wine and food. "What is the secret of your great strength?"

she kept asking him when she knew his judgement was befuddled.

"I can't tell you," Samson would reply. "God does not want me to reveal my secret. If I did, I would lose my strength immediately. I'd be as weak as one of your disease-ridden Philistine friends."

But Delilah kept on whispering, "What is your secret? Come now, tell me your secret."

At last, Samson got tired of the game. He wanted Delilah to say other things, sweet things just for his ears.

"I'll tell you, then. Just so we can talk about something else. If you were to tie me up with seven new bow strings, I would lose my strength."

"Liar," laughed Delilah, trying to hide her jubilation. She waited until Samson fell asleep in her arms. When he started snoring, she fetched seven bow strings and tied him up with them. Then she called some Philistine guards, who came and surrounded the Israelite.

"Samson," whispered Delilah urgently, shaking his shoulder. "Wake up. There are Philistines in the house!"

Samson leapt up, the bow strings snapping as his muscles bulged, and the Philistines found themselves flung across the room.

"You have tricked me," screamed Delilah. "I never want to see you again."

She left at once, ordering her servants to bar Samson from her chamber.

But a few days later she invited him to supper again.

"I have forgiven you your deceit," she cooed, making eyes at him as she poured more wine, "but today you must tell me your real secret."

"Weave my long hair into your loom," whispered Samson. "I will lose my strength just as surely as a bee after it has stung a child."

While Samson slept, Delilah fetched her loom and wove his long hair into it and then called the guards.

"Samson, sweetest, wake up! The Philistines have come."

Once more Samson leapt up and the loom fell apart as he yanked his hair free of it. Delilah was livid; this fortune was proving to be very difficult to earn.

The next day she invited Samson to supper again. She fed him a rich stew, sweet fruits, expensive wine. Pouring wine, she showed off her new dress.

"I love you," said Samson, pulling her close to him.

"I love you too," cooed Delilah. "But I cannot trust you, Samson. You lie to me and you make a fool of me in front of my friends."

"Don't tell me, you want to know my secret," laughed Samson. "Enough about secrets. Come here and comb my hair."

Delilah stood up, slapping away his hands, trying to control her annoyance.

"Tell me your secret."

"Why is my secret so important to you?" Samson asked. "You wouldn't like me if I was a weakling."

"It's not the secret itself – it's the fact that you don't trust me. How can two people love each other if there is no trust between them?"

"It's my hair, then, if it's so important for you to know. It has never been cut. If I were ever to chop off my locks, I'd lose my strength."

"I don't believe you."

"Delilah, don't torture me. I've told you the truth. Now come here and comb my hair."

Delilah returned to the cushions. She had a comb in her pocket and she started to run it through Samson's

thick, luxurious mane. Lulled by the wine, the combing, and Delilah's soft singing, Samson fell asleep. When he woke up again, he was being prodded roughly by the end of a spear.

"Wake up, Samson. The Philistines are here to get you."

He leapt up, ready to grab the nearest Philistine soldier. But something was wrong. The soldier slapped Samson's hands away as if he were a child. Delilah had shorn off his hair while he was asleep and he had lost his strength.

A crowd gathered outside Delilah's house. Israelite and Philistine gasped as the once great Samson was dragged to prison, squirming and bellowing. The Philistine judges sentenced him to a life of hard labour. He was blinded to make

sure he would not escape. Then he was lashed to the wheel of a mill, to grind corn like a donkey.

People came to stare at him and to poke fun. Samson, once respected and much-feared, had become a freak.

The Philistines worshipped many gods, but Dagon, the fish-god who protected their grain and their farmers, was their chief deity. Every year, a great festival was held in his honour, to thank him for the harvest and ask for protection from the weather. Samson was taken to their pagan temple in chains, with garlands of flowers hung around his neck as if he was to be a sacrifice on Dagon's altar.

Philistine soldiers chained him between two enormous pillars, his chains fastened to hoops close to the ceiling. Revellers swarmed around him, prodding, kicking and laughing at the great Israelite hero and cursing his people. Delilah was there too. He could hear her voice above the din of the crowds. He could picture her mingling with priests and generals, elders and judges. No doubt they had all come to the temple to worship and talk politics.

Samson lifted his blind eyes to the ceiling and prayed.

"Please, God, let me get my revenge. Favour me one last time. There is something I can do to help your people, your chosen nation…"

The wind rushed through the door of the temple, ruffling Samson's hair, and he knew that God had heard his prayer. In the long months he had been chained to the mill, Samson's hair had grown again, as thick and luxurious as ever. Perhaps all his mistakes had led him to this one place, this one moment in history. His destiny.

Stretching his scarred arms, Samson reached out to the pillars on either side of him. He had been in Dagon's temple before, with Delilah, and he knew that the whole ceiling rested on those two pillars. One mighty push in each direction and…

The priests looked up from their altar. They heard Samson's roar and the frightened screams of the crowd as the pillars started to collapse. Stones and bricks rained down. Dust stung everyone's eyes. Priests and worshippers, soldiers and generals, now as blind as Samson, ran and fought in a frantic bid to escape. No one survived. Dagon's mighty temple disintegrated in minutes, burying everyone inside it.

The Israelites found Samson's body under the debris, one hand poking out from the rubble. He was dead, but he had taken most of the Philistine leaders with him. Without their leaders to direct them, the Philistines were lost. Soon the Israelites would subdue them and regain the Promised Land…

Ruth and Naomi

"Do not press me to leave you . . .
Where you go, I will go; where you lodge, I will lodge;
your people shall be my people, and your God my God."

RUTH 1:16

East of Judah, across the Dead Sea, was a country called Moab. A family of Israelite refugees came to this land, a farmer called Elimelech, his wife Naomi and their two young sons, Mahlon and Chilion. They were escaping from the famine in Judah; the crops had failed for the third year on their little farm in Bethlehem.

The Moabites did not particularly like the Israelites, and the Israelites thought the Moabites were a sorry mob of idol-worshippers, praying to the strange gods of Baal. When God's chosen people were wandering in the desert, many young men had been lured into marriage by Moabite women.

Still, Elimelech and his family had no choice. It was either settle in Moab or starve. For a long time they worked hard, bringing in a better harvest each year. Then Elimelech died, leaving his young sons to look after the family.

Before Naomi knew it, the boys were grown-ups, working the land, trading animals, filling the house with their noise and their hopes and dreams. Brought up in Moab, they did not think the Moabites a sorry bunch. They both married local girls – Chilion to Orpah and Mahlon to Ruth.

After years of travel and toil, now life should have been easy for Naomi. But it was not to be. Her sons both died suddenly, like their father, leaving their wives sad young widows, their mother nearly mad with grief and loneliness.

"I must return to Judah," she said. "I must be among my people again. Someone there, a distant relative perhaps, will take pity on me and look after me."

"We are your family," cried Ruth and Orpah. "We will look after you, Mother."

Naomi shook her head.

"No, you two must marry again. You

need a man to look after you. A widow is nothing in this world – less than the dust men walk on. I'm too old to marry again – I can't have children."

"Then we will come with you to Judah," said Ruth.

"The Israelites hate Moabites, especially women. You would be persecuted – people would jeer at you as you went to the well, or the fields."

"But we can't let you travel on your own," said Orpah. "No, we will both come with you."

And so the three set out together on the long journey to Judah. They had many days walking ahead of them. But before long, Naomi spoke once more.

"You two must go back to your own country now. I'll be safe walking on my own from here."

"Very well," said Orpah, who had already started to miss her home and her friends, whom she sat with at the loom to weave shawls and blankets.

Ruth would not join her sister-in-law.

"I am staying with you, Mother," she insisted to Naomi. "Your country will be my country, your people, my people. I shall eat the food you eat and worship the god you worship. When I die, I shall be buried close to you."

Naomi could see that Ruth was determined to follow her. No amount of arguing was going to change her mind. The pair crossed the River Jordan and made their way slowly to Judah, across the hot, punishing desert. Soon they reached Bethlehem, Naomi's old village, just a small group of houses huddled together on a hill.

"We have come at a good time," said Ruth. "Look, it's harvest time. The farmers are reaping the barley."

As soon as Naomi was settled at an inn, Ruth hurried to the fields. There she joined the gleaners – orphans and widows who were allowed to pick the stray ears of corns missed by the sickle-wielding reapers. Ruth worked so hard picking the barley, that her veil was soon bulging with grain.

"Who is that woman?" asked the owner of the field, a middle-aged man named Boaz.

"She is a Moabite," sneered one of the harvesters, a hired hand. "She came to Israel with her mother-in-law, an old woman called Naomi."

"Make sure she gathers as much barley as she wants," snapped Boaz. "And do not insult her, even if she is a Moabite."

Naomi was a close relative of Boaz's. The rich farmer, a land-owner really, had heard she'd returned to Bethlehem a widow. But he hadn't realised she was destitute, relying on her daughter-in-law to scavenge for corn.

Back at the inn, Ruth showed Naomi the barley.

"You must have found favour with the land-owner," said Naomi.

That very same day she got to know that the field Ruth had been working in belonged to Boaz, a member of her own family. She also knew that Boaz was not married. Under Jewish law, he had a duty to wed Ruth, to provide for her and protect her. She was his relative, after all, entitled to all the rights decreed by Jewish law.

"Put on your best dress," said Naomi. "Tonight, find Boaz alone. He is guarding his harvest in the barn. Tell him that you have the right to marry him, according to the laws of this land."

"Ruth, that duty goes to your closest relative," said Boaz, when she found him in the barn. "You have another blood-relation, closer to you than I am, living just outside Bethlehem. You must marry him."

He said this with sadness, because he liked Ruth and was touched by her devotion to her mother-in-law.

Ruth tried hard to smile. She too liked Boaz and his gentle manner.

"Perhaps this relative is married already. If he has children he would not want to marry me too, because he would have to divide his property between too many heirs."

"I shall see him tomorrow," said Boaz.

At dawn, he hurried to the city gates, which had just been opened for the day. He waited by a well and before long, Ruth's other relative arrived with his sheep, ready to go out to the fields.

"A good morning to you, kinsman," said Boaz.

"A good morning to you, cousin."

Boaz explained about Ruth, the death of her husband and her journey to Bethlehem with Naomi.

"I'm afraid I cannot marry the girl," said the cousin. "I have too many people who depend on me

for their food and well-being. I cannot add more to my burden. Why don't you marry Ruth? If I denounce my right to her, she would be free to be your wife."

As he spoke, Boaz's relative took off one sandal. There were elders nearby, who met at the gates every morning to settle disputes between neighbours and traders. They watched Boaz's relative hand over the sandal – a sign that he was waiving his right to marry Ruth.

Boaz and Ruth married soon after the harvest had been stored. They settled happily in a house near Bethlehem. Naomi came to live with them, thanking God for his kindness. Soon Ruth was the proud mother of a child, a boy called Obed, who would grow up to be the grandfather of the Isrealite's greatest king.

Samuel

"Now the sons of Eli were scoundrels; they had no regard for the Lord or for the duties of the priests to the people . . . the sin of the young men was very great."

1 SAMUEL 2:12, 17

It was the first day of the harvest festival and the road to Shiloh was packed with people – people on donkeys, people in carts, people on foot and rich merchants on horses. Children carried bundles of food and jars of water.

Shiloh was the place where the Israelites kept the ark of the covenant, built by their ancestors to house the Ten Commandments. It was the place where they came each year to celebrate the end of the harvest, and where they came to worship, to ask God for anything they needed.

That was why Hannah had come to Shiloh; she wanted a child. She wanted more than anything else to be a mother. Her husband, Elkanah, had another wife called Peninnah, who had as many children as there were stones in the river, it seemed. Why couldn't Hannah have a child, just one?

"Give me a son," she prayed to God,

"and I promise I'll dedicate him to you. He'll live here, in the shrine at Shiloh, to serve you all his life."

God answered Hannah's prayer. She and Elkanah had a boy. They called him Samuel and, when he was still very young, they took him to Shiloh, to serve God at the temple. The high priest there was Eli, an old man with two grown-up sons. He took Samuel under his wing, gave him jobs to do and taught him to respect God.

"Who is this child, Father?" asked Eli's sons, Hophni and Phinehas, when at last they noticed Samuel.

"He is Samuel. God has called him to serve at the shrine."

"But Father, Hophni and I serve at the shrine. We will take over your work when you grow too old. Perhaps he can be our servant. We need someone to keep the temple clean."

Samuel, standing nearby, said nothing.

What Hophni and Phinehas were saying was true. They had been chosen to serve in the temple, to bring the people's offerings to the altar and advise the poor and the needy. Unfortunately it was said that they were not fit to enter the temple; that they stole food from the altar, forgot to pray and took people's offerings. So why had Samuel's mother brought him to the temple? How was he going to dedicate his life to God?

The answer came some time later, as Samuel lay on his sleeping mat in the

"I did not call," said the old priest. "You must have been dreaming. Go back to bed."

Samuel returned to his cot. He was sure he hadn't been dreaming. He had been awake, thinking of his mother, so far away from Shiloh.

"Samuel."

There it was again – the voice of the old priest calling. Perhaps he was becoming forgetful. Samuel rushed to his side.

"I am here, Master."

corner of the temple by the ark. Eli had grown blind, and so he had requested that the young boy sleep close by, in case he needed anything.

A voice made Samuel sit up.

"Samuel. Samuel."

He pushed aside the curtain separating him from Eli and dashed over.

"What do you need, sir?"

"It wasn't me."

"But Master, I definitely heard someone calling my name."

"I did not call out. I was praying."

Samuel returned to his mat, anxious and slightly scared. If it wasn't Eli calling him, then who was it? The voice was definitely in the temple. Perhaps it was a pilgrim, wanting his help. Or a thief.

But why would a thief draw attention to himself?

"Samuel."

There it was a third time. Now Samuel could hear noises too: Eli was reaching for his cane. He rushed to the old priest.

"I heard that voice again."

The old priest stood up shakily.

"Samuel, if you hear anyone calling you again, say, 'Speak, Lord, your servant is listening.'"

"I will." Samuel pulled the curtain across his little bed. He lay on his sleeping mat, eyes forced shut, waiting. Would the voice call again?

"Samuel."

Now he could tell it wasn't Eli calling. This voice was louder, deeper. He sat up.

"I am here, Lord, your servant is listening."

"Samuel," said the voice. *"Eli's children are not worthy of being my priests. I shall punish them and their duties shall be passed on to another. Behold, something is going to happen that will make Israel remember my power."*

At dawn, Samuel rushed to open the temple doors. Pilgrims were already gathering outside, eager to offer sacrifice.

"Samuel," said Eli, "did the voice speak again?"

Samuel blushed, trembled. How could he tell the old priest what God had said?

"Do not be afraid," said Eli. "I know that my children are not worthy to serve the Lord."

Then Samuel told him all that God had revealed and Eli blessed the boy, for he realised that Samuel had been chosen by God to serve Him. Samuel continued to listen to God – he grew up to be a great prophet and all the people of Israel listened when he told them what God said.

David and the Giant

Saul said to David, "You are not able to go against this Philistine to fight with him; for you are just a boy, and he has been a warrior since his youth."

1 SAMUEL 17:33

David was the great-grandson of Ruth and Boaz. A shepherd, like his brothers before him, David spent all day in the fields around Bethlehem, looking after his family's sheep and goats. Most people found tending sheep boring, but not David.

David knew how to amuse himself. While his flock munched on grass, he practised shooting pebbles from his sling. He knocked stones off walls or fruit off branches with just one shot. Sometimes he'd play his harp or sing the songs he heard from older shepherds or made up himself. Everyone said David was a good musician and a talented singer.

"Good enough to play for the king," said his father, Jesse.

The people of Israel had a king now. King Saul was a brave warrior who had led them into battle against the Philistines many times. Three of David's older brothers had joined the army to fight for Saul. David wished they would come home, to tell him all about the battles and help him move the sheep to greener hills.

There wasn't much chance of that. The Philistines were on the march again, stealing back Israelite land.

They were camped in the Valley of Elah, so the Israelite army was going there to fight them.

"Take this food and wine to your brothers," said Jesse to David. "It will remind them of home. The peaches are so succulent this year."

David took the sack of food, tied his harp to his back and hitched his sling over the cord around his waist.

When he arrived at the battlefield, he saw the Israelites were camped on one side of the valley and the Philistines on the other. A stream ran between the two armies – a clear trickle of water as yet unsullied with blood.

"When does the next battle start?" David asked, hoping to see some action.

"Who is our champion?" asked David.

His brothers shook their heads, laughing and slapping each other on the shoulder.

It soon became clear why no one from the Israelite camp would face the Philistine hero. He was a giant, ten feet tall. A man called Goliath. As he walked

"The armies are not fighting," replied one of his brothers. "It's champion against champion."

David knew what that meant. Sometimes, instead of making the armies fight, war generals would pit two champions against each other, one representing each army. The winner would claim victory for his side.

towards the enemy camp, the ground shook beneath his feet. When he bellowed, the birds in the nearby trees took flight, cawing in fright.

"Have none of you wretches the courage to face me? Forty times I have asked that one of you miserable maggots fight me, but you all refuse. Children of puny goats! Descendants of weaklings!"

"I'll fight him," said David.

"You?" laughed his brothers.

"Why not me? I might be small, but I have courage. God will be with me."

Word reached King Saul. A boy, a shepherd from Bethlehem, wanted to fight mighty Goliath. It was ridiculous – a joke really. How could a little shepherd boy even hope to scare a giant, let alone fell him? And yet something in King Saul, perhaps it was the voice of God, told him to trust this boy and to take him seriously.

"What makes you think you can win against this monster?" Saul asked the young shepherd when David was brought to him.

"I have fought animals that attacked my sheep," said David. "God was with me then. He will be with me now."

King Saul couldn't argue with that. If the boy wanted to fight, he would let him. There was no one else who would do it. He might not kill the giant, he might even get killed during the fight, but at least it would show the Philistines that the Israelites were not all cowards. King Saul ordered his men to dress David up in his own royal armour and give him the king's sword, heavy with gold and gleaming jewels.

David could not even lift it.

"I will suffocate in all this," he said. "I never wore armour to fight the wild animals that hounded my sheep and I will not wear it now. God will be my protection."

Barefoot, in his simple shepherd's clothes, David went out to face the giant, the enemy of Israel. He took only his sling with him and five pebbles from the nearby stream.

Goliath roared with laughter when he saw him.

"Going to wring my neck with your bare hands are you?"

"Today God will deliver you into my hands," said David.

Goliath barely heard him. The idea of the Israelites sending a boy to fight him was hilarious. It showed how desperate they were, how weaked by their losses on the field. The giant raised his spear. Its shaft was thicker than a man's wrist; its tip sharp and deadly. One throw, he thought, and he'd skewer the puny shepherd boy like a fish in the rapids.

On the other side of the stream, David put a pebble in his sling. He'd chosen a smooth pebble, rounded by years of lying in water. Squinting against the sun, he raised his weapon and twirled it above his head until it hummed. There was a whoosh as the pebble flew through the air, then a thunk as it hit Goliath's helmet.

For a moment the giant looked surprised. His eyes popped; a foolish grin spread across his lips. His right hand flew to his head, as if it were going to bat a wasp. Then he stiffened and keeled over like a tree being felled. He hit the ground with a crash, sending the birds up in a flap again. Shading his eyes with his hands, King Saul could see a trickle of blood running down the giant's helmet. David's pebble had pierced straight through Goliath's helmet and killed him instantly.

A cheer went up in the Israelite camp. The Philistines, shocked by the sudden death of their hero, turned and ran up the hill to their tents. The Israelites gave chase. God, they realised, was with them again. He'd sent a boy, a mere shepherd, to vanquish an unbeatable champion. The idea gave them new hope, new faith, new courage.

At last! Victory against their enemies was within reach!

David and Saul

*"Against whom has the king of Israel come out?
Whom do you pursue? A dead dog? A single flea?
May the Lord therefore be judge, and give
sentence between me and you."*

1 SAMUEL 24:14-15

The people of Israel sang David's praises. Such a courageous lad! So resourceful! Who would have thought that a little pebble could kill such a mountain of a man – Israel's mightiest foe? Saul invited David to stay at the palace, and introduced him to his beautiful daughter Michal and his son Jonathan.

Jonathan was older than David, but he was overawed by the hero who had felled the giant.

"Here, David,' he said, "take my armour and my cloak. This is my sword. Take it."

"You treat me like your brother," said David. He wanted to give Jonathan something too, but all he owned were the clothes on his back.

"Let's do everything together," laughed Jonathan. "We can hunt together, fight, even swim in the river."

The two swore a pact: they would be friends to the end.

"We will be blood brothers," said Jonathan, cutting their hands to seal the agreement with their blood.

"Brothers on earth, brothers in paradise," replied David.

Jonathan sister's Michal liked David too. In fact, she was in love with him. She said so to her friends and her servants and they told Saul.

"The whole country is in love with David," laughed King Saul. "He brings happiness to my house."

But one day, on the way home from a temple with his family, Saul overheard some women singing:

"Saul killed his thousands,
David his tens of thousands."

Instantly admiration turned to sour jealousy, love to bitter hatred. So the people thought that David was better than Saul? Perhaps they would want David to be the next king. Saul had never quite forgotten the rumours, brought to the city by countryfolk; Samuel, the prophet, had been seen pouring sacred oil on David's head, right there in the fields. Did God also want David to be the next king, perhaps before Saul had even died? Was the Lord angry with Saul because sometimes he had ignored his will?

The thought of losing his crown made Saul afraid. He swore to destroy David before he could take the throne. That very next day, unable to suppress his fury, he threw his spear at the young hero, right there in his throne room, in front of witnesses. David, who was playing his harp, jumped out of the way and the spear embedded itself in the wall behind him.

"It slipped in my hands," muttered Saul and he left the room.

"Father means to kill you, he is jealous of you." sobbed Jonathan to David.

"How could a king be jealous of a common man?" asked David.

"The people say God has chosen you to be the next king."

David remembered the day Samuel had poured sacred oil on his head. He had only been a young boy then.

David was ready to go into hiding, but Saul said he was sorry and that he would not try to harm David again. In time he gave David permission to marry Michal. A good job came with the marriage – the post of commander in the Israelite army. Saul secretly hoped David would get killed on the battlefield, his body trampled on by horses.

David wasn't killed. A brave fighter, he won skirmishes and inspired his men. The elders showered him with praise for his victories and the people loved him more and more.

"I hear David is very ill," said Saul to his soldiers one day. "Go to his house tonight and bring him here so that my doctors can treat him."

Michal told the soldiers that her husband was too sick to get up, so the soldiers carried the whole bed back to the palace. As soon as he saw it, Saul took out his knife and stabbed through the blankets.

"My own children plot against me!" he thundered as he found he harmed nothing but an idol, covered with clothes and blankets. "They've turned against their own family."

Michal had suspected that her father would make another attempt on David's life. At sunset, she had taken an idol, rolled it up in some cloth and tucked the disguised statue into their bed instead of her husband.

"Why do you want to kill David, father?" said Jonathan. "He is innocent. He is loyal to you."

"He is my enemy!" swore the King, his eyes brimming with tears of rage and hatred. "I shall hunt him down. I shall crush him under my foot like a poisonous snake – like the treacherous rat that he is."

Jonathan knew that Michal had smuggled David out of the house. He rode out to their hiding place in the fields, a spot where he and David had often hunted together.

"My father means to kill you," he told David. "Escape to the desert, my friend. I shall keep close to the king and I shall send you word as soon as I learn something that will help you."

The two friends hugged and cried on each other's shoulder. They repeated their pact of friendship and then David fled to the desert. Lots of people – farmers who'd lost their land, men on the run from Saul's guards, soldiers dismissed from the army – joined David. They swore to protect him forever and stay with him as outlaws; defending Israel from the Philistines, fighting their rich enemies and giving the spoils to the poor. The band came to a temple in Nod, in need of bread and water.

"I need a sword too," said David. "I left my house without a weapon."

"Here is a sword which once belonged to Goliath, the giant you killed," said the priest. "Take it."

David wiped the dried blood from its blade. Many years had passed since the battle with the giant. The young shepherd had grown up and could handle heavy weapons easily now. Saul pursued David around the country, from one hideout to another, through plain and desert and gated town. But he could not find him.

Once, hunting for David in the desert, Saul stopped to rest in a cave.

His guards built a fire to roast a deer. Deep in the bowels of the cave, a group of men sat still and listened to the crackle of burning twigs – it was David and his fugitives.

"Now is your chance to kill the king, to free yourself and us." whispered the outlaws to David.

David crept through the dark like a shadow. Slowly, he reached out to the king. His men were right. Here was the chance to kill Saul, to become free. But something stopped David from raising his sword. The man who lay unsuspecting before him was his best friend's father, his own father-in-law. He couldn't hurt the king, God's chosen ruler. It wasn't right. So he cut off a piece of Saul's robe instead.

In the morning, gripped by panic, Saul fled the cave. Who had crept up on the king unnoticed? Who had made

him a laughing stock in front of his guards? David followed the royal party, the piece of robe in his hand.

"Sire!" he called from his horse. "Here is a piece of cloth which I cut from your robe while you were resting. Now do you still believe that I wish to harm you?"

Perhaps he does not want to overthrow me after all, thought the king. Perhaps Jonathan is right. But the king's fears would not leave him, no matter how many times he prayed. He continued his war against David, until the young man was forced to escape to the land of the Philistines. David was living there when the Philistines marched on Israel once more. They thought that if Saul was attacking his own trusted men, they stood a chance of wiping out the Israelite army once and for all. There was a fierce battle on the slopes of Mount Gilboa. Blood ran on both sides, seeping deep into the earth.

David, returning from an expedition, waited for news. Who had won? Was his most trusted friend Jonathan alive? Had Saul been captured? A messenger arrived and threw himself at David's

feet; his face was covered in ashes, a sign of grief and mourning.

"The worst news, commander; the king's three sons were killed in battle last night. His Highness was wounded and killed himself before he could be captured, noble to his last breath. Even now, the enemy is hanging his armour from the city walls. The people are calling out your name. Sire. You are to be our next king. Hail, King of Israel."

David turned away from the messenger. Jonathan dead. His best friend gone!

His king too. What a price to pay to become king, if indeed God had chosen him to become the ruler of Israel. He fell to the ground, his body wracked with grief and tears. He might be the new king of the Israelities, but life without his best friend would never be the same again.

Wise King Solomon

*All Israel heard of the judgement that the king
had rendered; and they stood in awe of the king, because
they perceived that the wisdom of God was in him.*

1 KINGS 3:28

King David had many sons, but he chose Solomon, one of the youngest, to be his heir and to sit on his throne in Jerusalem and rule Israel when he died.

King Solomon was handsome – a talented hunter but a gentle soul. One night, after offering sacrifice on a hill top, the curtains around his bed billowed and Solomon heard the voice of God whispering to him.

"Solomon. I am pleased with your sacrifice of a thousand burnt offerings. Ask for anything and I shall give it."

Solomon answered without hesitation.

"God, you have put me in charge of a large nation – an empire. Please give me the wisdom to rule it well, to know right from wrong and to recognise good from bad."

God was pleased. Solomon had not asked for riches or fame, only wisdom, the greatest tool a king could need.

"I shall make you the wisest man in the world, Solomon. No one who lived before you and no one who shall come after you will be as wise as you. And I shall give you riches too, and fame. Your name will be an inspiration to people for the rest of time."

The curtains flapped against Solomon's face and he woke up.

"Lord?"

There was no answer, just the curtains billowing in the wind.

"I was dreaming," Solomon told himself. "It was only a dream."

He felt sad on his way to Jerusalem that morning. If only his dream about God had been real – if only he were wise and could rule over God's chosen people in a way that satisfied everyone. Kings lived in the lap of luxury, but they spent endless days agonising over hard decisions, wondering if their edicts and commands were the right ones.

The throne room was full of people that morning, seeking justice from their king. Two women were brought before him; both young mothers, both obviously poor and showing signs of distress.

"Sire," said one. "My friend and I share a room at an inn. God blessed us both with sons a few weeks ago. Last night, my friend's son died in his sleep, so she crept to my bed and took my child, leaving hers beside me."

"She is lying!" snapped the other woman. "It was her baby that died. I never went near her bed. Surely she would have heard me if I did?"

"I am not lying," wept the first mother. "When I got up in the morning, I found a baby limp and cold. But he wasn't my son. I could tell right away; he felt lighter in my arms. It was her son I was holding and my son was in her arms."

"Your majesty, she has lost her mind with grief," insisted the second woman. "That's why she wants my son."

Solomon looked from one woman to another. How sad, he thought, that close friends should be driven to enmity by the death of a child. But who was the real mother? Who was telling the truth?

"Help me be wise, God," murmured Solomon. "Give me the gift you promised in my dreams."

He called for the child. A guard brought the baby to him, gurgling in freshly-washed linen.

"You both want the baby," Solomon said to the women. "And I see no reason why you shouldn't both have a share of him. Bring him to me."

The guard stepped up to the throne, holding the baby out to the king as if it were a lamb to be sacrificed. Looking down at the wriggling form, Solomon took up his sword, polished that very morning by one of the servants.

"The baby will be cut in two," Solomon declared. "Both mothers shall have a half."

The first mother looked up at the king in horror, her face frozen with shock. She opened her mouth to speak, but the words seemed unable to pass her lips.

The second woman stood up. "The king has spoken. Justice must be done. We shall both have half a son."

"No," whispered the first woman, finding her voice. "Do not kill my child. Give him to her. Let her take him."

Solomon's sword stopped high above his head, its blade catching the light from the lamps around the temple. The baby, unaware of what was happening, started to gurgle. His feet kicked backwards and forwards. Solomon handed his sword to the guard and took the infant in his arms.

"You are the real mother," he said, walking down to the first woman. "No mother wants her own child to be harmed."

And as he spoke, he placed the baby gently in her arms.

"It is my child," whimpered the second woman. "I want it. A woman is nothing in this world without a son. How can I live without him?"

Solomon turned to her, pity showing on his face.

"Pray to God for forgiveness," he said, "because you have lied to your friend and to your king. Perhaps he will give you another child who will look after you in your old age."

As the two women left, the first one hugging her baby, covering his little face with kisses, Solomon sat back on his throne. All around him, the elders and priests, the soldiers and ambassadors from other countries looked at him in awe. They had never seen a king solve a problem with such insight, such tenderness. Solomon was truly the wisest ruler in the world.

The wind rippled the curtains of the throne room and Solomon heard God's voice again.

"Ask anything, Solomon, and I will make it come true."

Elijah and the Prophets

Now Elijah... said to Ahab, "As the Lord
the God of Israel lives, before whom I stand, there shall be
neither dew nor rain these years, except by my word."

1 KINGS 17:1

Solomon was a wise and popular king who built a magnificent temple in Jerusalem to house the ark of the covenant. But his many foreign wives led him into sinful ways. His wife from Sidon wanted an altar erected for her goddess, Ashtoreth. His wife from Ammon wanted a temple built for her god, Milcon. And his wife from Moab, not to be outdone, wanted Solomon to offer sacrifice to her god, Chemosh. Solomon agreed to it all.

God was angry. His chosen king had turned away from him and broken the agreement his ancestors had made with God in the desert.

"I shall take your kingdom away from you and your family," God thundered, his voice assaulting Solomon's ears during a storm. *"I shall give it to your servant. Only one small part of it will remain in your son's hand, for the sake of his grandfather David, my beloved."*

God's words came true. After Solomon's death, the country was torn in two by civil war. In the south, in Judah, only two tribes remained loyal to Rehoboam, Solomon's son. In the north, the other ten, the majority of Israel, chose another king to rule them. He was Jeroboam, once one of Solomon's court officials. Jeroboam built golden bulls for the people to worship, like the one the Israelites had prayed to near Mount Sinai. He ordered a festival, in honour of the bulls, and offered sacrifice at their altars himself.

God sent prophets, stern holy men, to warn the people of Israel to change their wicked ways. But the people ignored them. One evil king succeeded another, and each one brought new gods to Israel, new idols to worship. King Ahab favoured Baal, because his wife Jezebel was a devout follower. She made Ahab build a temple to Baal, so she could offer sacrifice whenever she wanted to. God's prophets begged Ahab to turn back to God and denounce Baal, but Jezebel had them all put to death.

At last God's patience ran out. He sent the prophet Elijah to deliver a message.

"God has seen your evil ways and he is going to punish you," Elijah said to King Ahab and his people. "There will be no rain in Israel until the true God of Israel says there will be."

Ahab and Jezebel laughed in Elijah's face. The court tittered and nudged each other.

But they started to get worried when, month after month, the sky remained clear and no rain fell. Jezebel prayed to Baal, Ahab offered sacrifice, but it was no use. The sky stayed blue, the sun blazing down on the fields, withering the crops with its fierce glare.

"Kill Elijah," hissed Jezebel. "Destroy that prophet of doom – let's see if his god will save him."

But the old man could not be found. God had told him to go into hiding, somewhere remote and safe. Three years later, God told him it was time to return to the king.

"Why are you here?" demanded King Ahab. "Has your god not done enough to destroy Israel? The rivers are dry, the streams have vanished. Every day people are dying of hunger."

whole country. He went there to talk to God and to enjoy the view of the hills and sea. Early the next day, hundreds of people, summoned by Ahab's messengers, gathered on Mount Carmel to see this contest between God and Baal. King Ahab came too, riding in his magnificent chariot. He was

"It is you who is destroying the land of Israel," said Elijah. "You have turned God's people away from him."

"Baal is the real god, old man," spat Queen Jezebel.

"If Baal is the real god, then let him prove it," Elijah challenged her. "Summon the people of Israel and the prophets of Baal to Mount Carmel tomorrow morning."

Mount Carmel was a mountain over looking the sea, lush with oak and carob trees. It was Elijah's favourite spot in the

accompanied by no less than four hundred and fifty prophets of Baal, sent by Queen Jezebel. The sound of their chanting carried on the wind.

Elijah, waiting for them on a ridge, watched the crowds come. In a pen behind him were two bulls, their horns gleaming in the rising sun.

"It is time you decided who to follow: the true God or Baal," Elijah said to the people. "Look, I have brought bulls for the sacrifice. Let the prophets of Baal, all four hundred and fifty of them, kill a bull and place it on the altar. Then let them ask Baal to send them fire, to burn the sacrifice, and we'll see if he answers their prayer."

The prophets of Baal built an altar of felled trees, chanting as they worked. They killed one of the bulls and dragged its huge carcass on to the wood.

At last Elijah held up his hand. While the priests of Baal had been dancing, Elijah's assistants had built another altar. It was made of twelve large stones – one boulder for each tribe of Israel. Elijah scattered wood and kindling on the altar. The bull was laid on it, its eyes staring at the sky. Elijah poured

Looking up to the sun, the symbol of their god, the source of his power, they started dancing.

"Oh Baal, lord of lords, giver of life and harvests, set this sacrifice alight. Show the people of Israel that you are their true god."

The sun shone brighter, a hot wind blew across the mountain, but no fire came from the sky, no burning ember escaped the sun. The priests danced faster. Their voices got louder. They tore off their robes and beat their chests.

water on the bull, soaking it along with the wood and the stones so it would be almost impossible to set light to it. Then he held up his hands.

"Oh Lord, God of Abraham, of Isaac and Israel. Let it be known today that you are the one true God."

As the prophet spoke, a fiery flash of lightning shot down from the heavens. The people gasped. The wet kindling on the altar started to hiss. Steam rose out of the wood and within seconds the bull was burning and the altar began to crumble. The people fell to their knees, howling with fear.

"Oh Lord, you are the one true God, our God, the God of Israel."

The prophets of Baal, rightly fearing for their lives, gathered up their tattered robes and ran down the mountain.

"Go back to your palace," Elijah said to King Ahab, "and tell your servants to prepare – the rains are coming."

Even as the king's chariot thundered down the mountain, clouds gathered in the sky. Soon it started to rain, the fat droplets pelting down from the sky.

The king's horses slipped around on the wet road. By the time he arrived at the palace, Ahab was soaked to the skin.

Elijah, almost wild with ecstasy, danced through the rain right up to the door of the king's palace. But he did not go in. Jezebel, he knew, would soon send soldiers to kill him, to silence him. He'd have to become a fugitive, wandering from one place to another, dodging her assassins. The prospect did not worry Elijah. He had done his work: the people of Israel had turned to God again.

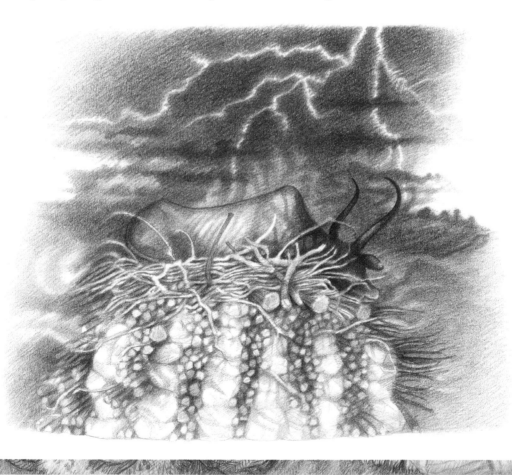

Elisha and the Child

As they continued walking and talking,
a chariot of fire and horses of fire separated the two of them,
and Elijah ascended in a whirlwind into heaven.

2 KINGS 2:11

Elijah was getting old. King Ahab had died but his wife Jezebel was very much alive and was still crying out for the prophet's blood. Her followers still worshipped Baal, offering sacrifices in his temples and blessing his name.

Elijah had chosen a young prophet, Elisha, to continue his war against the false gods and to deliver God's message.

When Elijah knew his time had come to die, he visited some of his friends and other prophets living in Jericho. Then he took Elisha for a walk on the banks of the River Jordan.

"This is my last journey," said Elijah to the young prophet. "Let me lean on your shoulder."

As he spoke, he rolled up his cloak and struck the waters of the river. A stiff breeze moved the reeds, and the water level fell, allowing the two prophets to cross to the opposite side.

"Ask what I can do for you before God sends for me," said Elijah.

Elisha could feel the breeze getting stronger, turning into a wind. He could

"you will know your request has been granted and God's power is with you."

Shivering, Elisha wrapped his cloak around his shoulders. The wind got stronger and suddenly, out of the clouds, a chariot of fire appeared.

see their friends, the holy men, watching from the other side of the river. He knew something astonishing, some kind of miracle, was going to happen.

"Elijah, leave me your power," he begged the prophet.

"If you see me depart," said Elijah,

It swooped towards them, flames leaping from it.

Elisha ducked, covering his eyes, and when he looked up again, his master had been swept into the chariot.

Within minutes the chariot had disappeared, leaving only Elijah's cloak on the ground. Elisha picked it up. He had seen Elijah depart this earth so he knew that God *had* given him the power to continue his work. Rolling up the cloak, Elisha struck the water in the river, just as Elijah had done. The water moved, creating a path for him across the riverbed. Yes, he thought, God is with me. The prophets on the banks of the Jordan fell to their knees and bowed before him.

A man called Gehazi became Elisha's servant. He brought a donkey, and the pair travelled around the countryside, helping the poor, bringing hope to the sick, praying with the needy. Their names became known all over Israel and wherever they went, people flocked to hear Elisha speak.

In Shunem, a tiny village near Galilee, a woman came out to meet them.

"You must be tired and hungry. My husband and I would be honoured if you dined with us tonight."

The woman and her husband were rich. They had a big house, fields and fine-woven clothes to wear.

"You must come again," they said to Elisha. "We shall build a room for you, so you will have somewhere you can call home."

The prophet was touched by the couple's kindness and wanted to give them something in return.

"They have everything they want in life," said Gehazi, "except the most important thing – a child of their own."

Elisha called the woman to him and said, "By this time next year, you will have a son."

Elisha's words came true. The woman gave birth to a child, a boy. She and her husband watched in delight, thanking God and Elisha as he grew from a baby to a young lad, running in the fields, playing with his friends and coming in late for supper and bed.

But one day, the boy was helping his father in the fields, when he put his hands to his head in pain.

"Why are you swaying, Father?"

"I am not swaying, Son."

"You are turning green, Father…"

The farmer rushed to his child, took him up in his arms. The boy was tottering and shivering with cold, even though it was a hot day. Sweat poured down his face.

"Mother!"

The woman ran out of the house, cloak flying behind her. Taking her son in her arms, she rushed to the prophet's room, but Elisha was nowhere to be found. It was too late. Her son was dead, the fierce heat of the summer sun had killed him.

"Saddle my donkey," she ordered her servants, laying her son's body on the prophet's bed.

She rode out across the fields, along the hills of Galilee, asking everyone she met, "Have you seen Elisha the prophet? Do you know where he is?"

By the time she got home, with Elisha following on Gehazi's donkey, the boy's body was cold and his joints stiff. Elisha asked everyone to leave his room.

In the dark, kneeling on the floor, he prayed to God. Then he got up, put his lips to the boy's mouth and breathed into it.

Outside, the woman heard her boy cough once, twice. Elisha's voice rose in prayer. The boy coughed again and again. After the seventh cough, the woman could stand it no longer. She rushed into the room, hardly able to take in the scene before her.

Her boy's eyes were open, shining, his skin flushed. He smiled at her.

"Mother!"

"Thank you," the woman whispered to Elisha, scooping the child in her arms, covering his face with kisses. Her husband and servants ran to the room, whooping with joy, sending the doves in the yard flapping up into the darkening sky.

"Do not thank me – thank the God of Israel," said Elisha, and he left the family alone to enjoy God's miracle. There was still a lot of work for a prophet of God to do in the country.

Daniel in the Lions' Den

Then the king gave the command, and Daniel was brought and thrown into the den of lions. The king said to Daniel, "May your God, who you faithfully serve, deliver you!"

DANIEL 6:16

Despite the prophets' warnings, the people of Israel still worshipped false gods and still refused to obey God's laws. So God allowed King Nebuchadnezzar and his army, who came from a land called Babylon, to punish the Israelites.

Daniel, a youth from Judah, watched in horror as the Babylonians laid siege to Israel, burning and looting towns and villages. They set fire to the city, destroyed Solomon's magnificent temple and looted its treasure and fine furnishings. When they left, they dragged many people back to Babylon with them, as slaves and prisoners-of-war. Some of Daniel's friends escaped with their families to nearby countries like Egypt and Moab. But Daniel did not manage to flee; he was captured and taken to Babylon to serve in King Nebuchadnezzar's palace.

Daniel was a clever young man. He still worshipped the God of Israel and he knew that God would rescue his people from exile one day, when they had learnt to obey the covenant. He grew from a servant to an advisor to King Nebuchadnezzar.

Years passed and a king called Belshazzar came to the throne. One night, Belshazzar held a banquet. There were enemies outside his city, trying to starve him out. Well, he would show them. He held a feast for a thousand officers, plying them with the best food and the costliest wine. It was the holy day of Bel Marduk, god of Babylon. Belshazzar's officers needed to remember how powerful Marduk was, what a great empire he'd given his followers. No foreign king was going to take that away from them.

"Use the golden cups and dishes King Nebuchadnezzar removed from the temple in Jerusalem," he ordered.

The goblets were brought. Wine was poured into them and offered up to Bel Marduk, god of Babylon. The guests drank deeply, ate delicious food and watched dancers whirl around the magnificent banquet room.

"I have never seen such a spectacle before," said a general. "Look at that hand, floating in the air, disembodied. How do your magicians perform such wizardry, sire?"

Everyone stared at the hand. It was writing a message on the wall – a scrawl they could not read. King Belshazzar turned pale, his cup slipping from his hands. This was no conjuring trick – the hand was real. It had obviously been sent by some god, to deliver a message.

"Who can read this?" he cried. No one spoke up, no one volunteered.

"Call for Daniel," said Belshazzar's mother. "I remember he interpreted King Nebuchadnezzar's dreams once. He is old but he might understand these strange words."

Daniel was interrupted in his prayers and taken to the banquet hall.

"Tell me what that writing means," ordered Belshazzar, "I will make you

rich if you do. I shall give you the finest purple cloak for your shoulders and a chain of pure gold will be hung around your neck. Indeed, I shall make you my prime minister, third in command over the entire kingdom."

"Alas," replied Daniel, looking at the writing, "you will have no need of a prime minister tomorrow. You have dishonoured God by using his cups to toast your false deities and he is going to take your kingdom from you."

Daniel was right. That very same night the Medes and the Persians entered Babylon through the water systems that flowed under the city. In the battle that followed, Belshazzar was killed.

Babylon had a new ruler – Darius the Mede. The new king chose leaders to look after the regions of Babylonia. Three wise men were selected to counsel the rulers. One of the three was Daniel, who quickly became a trusted advisor of the king. Daniel was allowed to keep his house and even to worship his own god.

Some of the leaders were angry and jealous – an Israelite slave to rule over them! To advise them! Why not a Mede, or a Persian, or even a Babylonian – someone who knew the local culture and customs? Thinking Daniel was now weak and old, they hatched a plot to kill him.

"Sire," one of them asked King Darius, "why don't you test the people to see how obedient they are to you? They look to their gods and prophets for guidance, but they should be turning to you."

Darius passed a law. For thirty days no one was allowed to pray to their god. Anyone who needed anything, no matter how important or trivial, had to come to the king. Refusal to obey the law meant instant death.

Everyone in the land obeyed. Temples were shut, statues of gods covered with sheets of expensive cloth. Only Daniel shrugged off the new law. He insisted on praying three times a day, his face turned towards Jerusalem, kneeling at his window as if he didn't care whether his enemies saw him or not.

"Sire," whispered the officials. "Daniel has disobeyed you; he is worshipping his own god even as we speak."

The king was heart-broken. How could his favourite advisor disobey him? Then the king realised he had been duped – his officers had known Daniel would continue to pray to his god. King Darius wished he could pardon the prophet and excuse his behaviour, but he didn't want to appear weak. Once made, a law could never be changed. Everyone had to obey it and those who did not had to suffer the consequences, including Daniel.

Guards came for Daniel and threw him in a pit where hungry lions were kept. King Darius retreated to his room, worrying and fretting. He could hear the lions roaring angrily in the dungeons – they were going to tear his friend limb from limb.

In the morning, the king crept out of bed. Pulling a cloak round his shoulders, he descended alone to the dungeons. It was too late to save Daniel, but the king would arrange to have the bones of the prophet taken and buried with full honours.

As he approached the pit, Darius heard a voice whispering prayers. There were no roars from lions – no gnashing of teeth or smacking of lips. The king looked down into the lion's den. It was unbelievable! In the pit below, Daniel was alive, sitting on the ground with the ferocious animals lounging near him like docile kittens.

"Sire," said Daniel, standing up. "God has protected me. He knew I had not wronged you."

"Your god is truly remarkable," said Darius. "His power is greater than any other god's."

He ordered his guards to throw the officials who had hatched the plot against Daniel into the lions' den. Then King Darius passed a new law: everyone in the kingdom was to bow down to Daniel's God, the true God.

Queen Esther

"Let my life be given me — that is my petition — and the lives of my people . . . we have been sold, I and my people, to be destroyed, to be killed, and to be annihilated."

ESTHER 7:3-4

The news raced through Babylon, making people at the markets drop their baskets, sending others running through the streets, telling every person they met.

"The exile is over! The king has said any Israelites who want to be free can go home to Israel, to rebuild Jerusalem!"

In Babylon, the Israelites had seen the error of their ways. They had returned to God and this was their reward – freedom in their own land. Forty-two thousand people collected their belongings right away, then saddled their horses and their mules. They set out on the long journey home. What joy! What hope for the future! The temple in Jerusalem would be raised again and the city fortified. Israel would be a great nation again.

Still, many Israelites had no wish to return to a run-down land, to start rebuilding Jerusalem. They wanted to be free, yes, but free somewhere else, a place with wealth and opportunity. They moved to different cities, set up new communities, joining others whose ancestors had been scattered during the invasion of Israel.

Many settled in Susa, the city of King Xerxes. Xerxes was more than a king really – his empire stretched all the way from India to Ethiopia in Africa. His city was teeming with traders and merchants. There were jobs to be had there, chances to get rich.

Xerxes loved holding feasts, giving lavish banquets that impressed princes and ambassadors alike. Always he called his queen Vashti to his table, to show off her grace and beauty. But one day Vashti refused to come. She was tired of being put on show, exhibited like a dumb animal at the market.

Xerxes was furious. How dare his wife let him down in front of dignitaries, men of rank? He stripped the proud Vashti of her crown and her titles.

"I shall have a new queen," he thundered. "One who will be only too happy to grant my wishes."

Princes and courtiers, servants and vassals were sent all around the empire to look for a suitable young woman to be the next queen. She had to be beautiful, she had to be wise, and most of all she had to have a desire to please the king.

"I know a woman who could be an excellent queen," thought Mordecai, an Israelite exile living in Susa. He hurried home to talk to Esther, his orphaned cousin who was in his care.

"Come to the palace," Mordecai said to Esther. "Perhaps you will be the next queen. But don't tell anyone you are an Israelite. Lots of people in Susa don't like us and they might hold your race against you."

Esther, dressed in her best robes, joined the other women at court. The palace was buzzing with expectation.

Who would the king choose to be his new queen? Who would be the lucky woman? Without hesitation, Xerxes chose Esther. He was besotted with her the moment he laid eyes on her. She was beautiful and graceful, answering all his questions with quiet confidence.

Esther sent word to her wise cousin without delay.

"Cousin Mordecai, I have been chosen – I am the new queen!"

Mordecai returned her message with another important one; "Esther, I've just heard two guards plotting to kill the king. You must inform him at once."

When Esther told Xerxes, he had the guards executed and thanked Mordecai for his loyalty and courage. The king promised him a reward and had the royal scribes write Mordecai's name in the royal record books.

Then a new Chief of Staff arrived in the palace, a man called Haman. The moment he arrived, he made new regulations for the king's household.

"I expect everyone to treat me with respect," he said. "When I appear at the palace gates in the morning, all the staff must bow down to me."

Mordecai refused to obey the new rule. He bowed down only to praise his own God. Haman was livid when he found out. How dare a lowly palace worker, an Israelite, make him look like a fool in front of the whole household?

He swore to have the old man killed. Better than that, he would have all the Israelites in Susa killed. That would show everyone how powerful he was.

"There is a nation, a group of foreigners in this city, which refuses to obey your laws and mocks them in the market place," Haman lied to Xerxes. "Let me put these rebels to death."

The king nodded, his mind distracted by more important matters. Haman had not said which group of people were refusing to obey his laws and Xerxes did not ask. His empire was teeming with foreigners and slaves, what did it matter if a few perished in order to teach others a lesson? He handed Haman his seal.

"Tell the scribes to write the edicts. These people will be put to the sword."

A few nights later, Esther heard people weeping outside the palace. Her cousin approached her with trembling hands.

"Esther, you must speak to the king," begged Mordecai. "Save your people and yourself. We have been falsely accused of treason and we are to die."

What was Esther to do? How could she reverse the decision of a mighty ruler, when to even approach him without his permission would mean death? Quickly, the queen prepared a banquet in her chambers – a dinner for three. She invited Xerxes and Haman, the new chief of staff.

Xerxes was dazzled when he arrived

for the meal. Esther looked beautiful in her silk robes and jewels, with her hair in ringlets and her big eyes outlined with kohl.

"Tell me what you want, my queen," he said, "and I will grant your wish."

"Come again tomorrow," said Esther, "and I will tell you what I want."

That night, Xerxes could not get Esther out of his mind. He had seen her talking to Mordecai at the palace gates. The king remembered how the old man had saved his life and realised he had never been rewarded.

"How would you reward someone who is loyal to you?" he asked Haman, wondering what he could give old Mordecai. Haman thought that the king was talking about him – after all, Haman was a true and loyal subject.

"Give him one of the royal robes, sire, and a horse with the royal crest on its head. Then have the guards escort him through the streets of Susa, declaring him a hero."

"A noble gift," agreed Xerxes. "See to it that the Israelite Mordecai gets all these honours."

Haman fumed when he heard the name. Mordecai – his enemy! Honoured instead of him! The chief of staff had already built gallows to hang the old man. He wanted to see him swing at the end of a rope, not be escorted by a guard-of-honour through the streets.

That evening, at Esther's second banquet, Haman was still angry and upset. The queen looked even lovelier than she had the night before – her skin glowed, her eyes shone. She moved with the grace of a swan.

"My lovely queen, tell me what you want," said the king again. "I promise to make it come true."

To his surprise, Esther threw herself at his feet.

"Please spare me my life, your majesty, that I might look after you for the rest of my days!"

"Spare your life?" cried Xerxes, sitting up on his couch. Who had ever mentioned killing the queen? She was the apple of his eye.

"I am an Israelite," said Esther, "and my life will be taken along with those of my countrymen. We have been falsely accused of refusing to obey your laws."

The king glared at Haman.

"Are the Israelites the people you meant to kill?" he asked.

Haman could only nod, his mind in a spin. He could feel the walls of the palace closing in on him – he had never guessed that Esther was an Israelite.

"Sire, my servants tell me Haman has built gallows for my cousin Mordecai. He will be the first to go to his death."

"Mordecai saved my life," said Xerxes. "He is no traitor. Guards, take Haman to the gallows he made and put him to death. My second in command shall be Mordecai. I trust him completely."

The king issued a new law that night. He could not change the first law, but to rescue the condemned Israelites he gave them permission to defend themselves.

And they did, in a battle with Xerxes' own soldiers. When the fighting had ended, Mordecai sent messengers all around the empire. The Israelites were to hold a two-day festival called Purim, to celebrate God's protection of his people and to honour Esther, the brave Israelite Queen.

Jonah and the Whale

"Pick me up and throw me into the sea; then the sea will quieten down for you; for I know it is because of me that this great storm has come upon you."

JONAH 1:12

God kept sending prophets to the Israelites to deliver his wishes, warnings and instructions. Only one prophet disobeyed him – Jonah.

Jonah was a timid man who lived in a small village. His name meant 'dove', and he preferred birds to people. He liked the simple way they lived, flying in the sunshine, pecking for food whenever they got hungry, never having to worry about tomorrow.

Then one day, Jonah heard a voice.

"Jonah, I want you to be my prophet."

Jonah dropped the bundle of sticks he was carrying.

"Me? A prophet?"

"Yes. Go to Nineveh. The people there are wicked. Tell them if they don't repent, I shall destroy the city."

Jonah started to tremble. Nineveh wasn't even an Israelite city – it was Assyrian. The capital of the Assyrian empire, in fact. The people there would never listen to a lowly Israelite, even if he claimed he was a prophet of God. Come to think of it, they would probably laugh at him, maybe even throw him in jail or behead him. Jonah had heard that the Assyrians were terrifying, and they hated the Israelites.

"*Jonah,*" thundered God's voice, making the reeds bend in the wind. "*Hurry – the people of Nineveh do not have much time.*"

Jonah returned home and collected the things he needed for the journey: bread, a goatskin of water, good sandals and a knife to defend himself.

But he did not set out for Nineveh. Instead, Jonah sneaked down the coast to the port of Joppa, hoping God was not watching and reading his intentions. He found a ship going to Tarshish, a city right across the Mediterranean Sea. Perhaps God would find someone else to be a prophet when He realised how far from Nineveh Jonah was.

The fare to Tarshish was costly; Jonah's pocket was empty by the time he'd handed all the silver to the captain. But he smiled to himself when the anchor was pulled out of the water.

"I'm getting away," thought Jonah happily. The sun beat down on the ship, warming the deck under his feet.

"I hope this good weather keeps up," said a sailor. "We'll reach Tarshish a day earlier than planned."

But the fine weather did not last. God knew Jonah was trying to escape him. In the afternoon, dark clouds built up in the sky, towering over the ship. A fierce wind filled the sails, making the rigging creak. Before long, a terrible storm was lashing the ship, tossing it high on mighty waves.

"It's my fault," Jonah shouted above the wind. "I am running away from God – disobeying his orders."

The sailors stared at him in horror.

"Throw me overboard!" shouted Jonah. "Get rid of me, or your ship will sink under God's wrath."

"No," said the captain. "You have paid your fare. I have a duty to take you safely to Tarshish."

But the gale blew harder, tearing at the sails. Waves pounded the deck, sweeping barrels and rope and sacks into the sea. Desperate, the sailors pushed Jonah overboard. He fell headlong, screaming with guilt and fear, and disappeared into the churning waves. The water closed over his head, sucking him down into the swirling, freezing depths.

When Jonah surfaced, spluttering and spitting salt-water, the waves had already started to subside. The wind was dropping.

"The ship is safe," said Jonah to himself with relief. "The sailors will live to see their families back home."

He raised his hand to wave, but suddenly he was plunged in the darkness again. Jonah found himself falling down a well of some kind, his feet and arms bumping against a rough wall. Not a hard stone wall but a soft, warm one. Regaining his feet, Jonah looked around him. There was light coming from a round hole high above him.

"It's a blowhole," cried Jonah. "I have been swallowed by a whale. I'm trapped inside this huge beast!"

He huddled on the quivering floor.

"I am sorry for disobeying you, God," he prayed. "If you spare me, I shall do your bidding. I shall go to Nineveh and deliver your warning to the people of Assyria."

The light in the round hole above him went out. The whale swam faster and faster through the stormy ocean, diving down for a time and then returning to the surface. By the end of the third day, Jonah was hungry and tired, shivering with cold.

"God," he cried, "are you there?"

Suddenly light flooded all around him. He felt the pulsating floor below him heave. Suddenly there was a loud noise. A moment later he was sailing through the air, head over heels. He landed on soft sand. The whale had thrown him up on a beach.

Fishermen came running to the aid of this poor soul, their children following close behind them.

"Are you hurt?"

They were speaking a language Jonah could understand – he could not be far from Israel.

"*Jonah*," whispered God's voice, his words as soft at the waves around the prophet's feet. "*Go to Nineveh. Tell the people there I am displeased with them.*"

They have forty days to repent or they shall perish."

"I will go, Lord," groaned Jonah.

He waited for his robe and sandals to dry. Then Jonah set out with little food or water, trusting that God would provide for him. His destination was truly Nineveh this time. Eventually Jonah reached Nineveh, tired but determined to do exactly as the Lord had commanded.

"Repent," he preached at the market. "People of Nineveh, turn to the Lord or He will punish you."

To his surprise the people listened, and returned with friends and relatives. Guards turned up at the market where he was speaking, but not to carry him away in chains. They took him to the king's palace, where the royal family was waiting, eager to meet the prophet. Servants set dishes of food before him and gave him new sandals for his tired feet. The king listened to every word Jonah said and trembled at the thought of God destroying his wonderful city.

"Tell him that we repent," he said. "Tell him we shall sin no more."

The king took off his royal robes and put on a sackcloth. He ordered everyone in the city to do the same and to fast.

"No one shall eat or drink," the king proclaimed, "until we have shown God we are sorry for our sins."

Jonah told God what the king had said, whispering into the desert breeze outside the city walls.

"*I shall not destroy Nineveh,*" came God's reply, "*for the people have obeyed my command.*"

Jonah should have been delighted – he had saved the lives of thousands, turned them all to God. But instead, he grimaced with anger.

"Now that you will not make the city walls tremble, the ground shudder under people's feet, they will never know I was speaking the truth. These people are the enemies of Israel, why have you forgiven them so easily?"

God asked Jonah, "*Have you any right to be angry?*"

The prophet said nothing, instead he made himself a shelter under an old tree, wincing at the intense heat.

"If only I could find some shade. This tree is dead, its branches bare."

He closed his eyes, trying to remember what the sea breeze in Joppa had felt like on his skin. Suddenly he smelt something fragrant that reminded him of his mother's garden at home. He opened his eyes – a vine with broad green leaves had spread over the dead tree. He was sitting in its shade; the leaves keeping the sun from his eyes.

"Thank you, God." He closed his eyes and went to sleep. The sun set and a full moon rose in its place. Jonah did not stir; his work in Nineveh had tired him out.

When he woke up again, the sun was burning his arms and legs. Worms had chewed up every leaf on the plant, leaving it as bare as the old tree.

"God, why did you let the plant die? I do not understand. It was such a beautiful plant."

"*If you are sad for a vine, a plant,*" replied God, his words tumbling through the branches, "*imagine how I would feel if I had to destroy the people of Nineveh.*"

"You are right, Lord," said Jonah.

He stood up and, dusting off his new sandals, Jonah set off on his way again. Now he understood – God loved the people of Nineveh, as he loved all people everywhere.

Soon people across Israel and beyond had heard of the prophet Jonah who tried to escape from the Lord's will, only to be brought back and given a second chance.

In the beginning

was the Word, and the Word was with God,

and the Word was God. He was in the

beginning with God. All things came

into being through him, and without him

not one thing came into being.

What has come into being in him was life,

and the life was the light of all people.

The light shines in the darkness, and

the darkness did not overcome it.

John 1:1-5

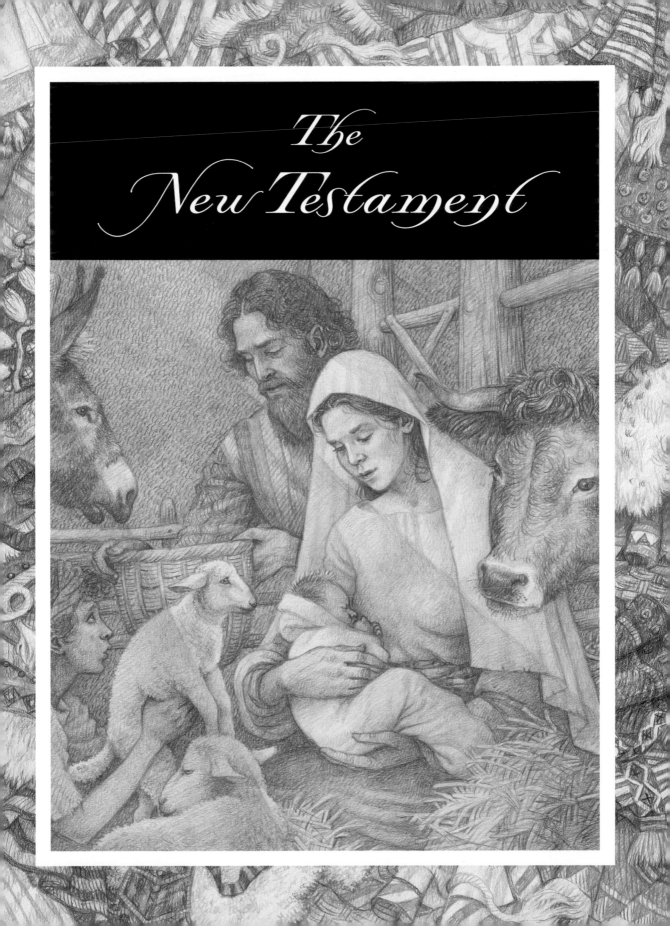

The New Testament

Mary and the Angel

The angel said to her, "Do not be afraid, Mary, for you have found favour with God. And now you will conceive . . . and bear a son, and you will name him Jesus."

LUKE 1:30–31

The news spread around the little town of Nazareth like wild fire – there was to be a wedding. What joy! What happiness! Mary was to marry Joseph, the carpenter. The bride-to-be had been seen at the well, wearing a veil, a sure sign that she was promised to someone. Joseph had spoken to her parents, they had talked to Joseph's family and together an agreement had been reached. Mary sat embroidering the dress she would wear on her wedding day. She was in her mid-teens, the perfect time for a girl to marry. Joseph, the village carpenter, was well over twice her age. Too old for Mary, some of her friends had said. They wanted her to marry someone closer to their own age, someone who could share jokes with them.

But Mary had known the moment she laid eyes on Joseph, that he was the one for her. He would be her husband, the man who would look after her and be the father to her children.

Sitting on her thin bedroll, Mary heard a rustle of wings, a faraway tinkle of shepherd bells, and looked up from her embroidery. A man, tall and broad-shouldered, was standing in her room, bathed in golden sunlight from the window.

"Hail, Mary. The Lord is with you."

What kind of words were these? Who was this stranger and how had he got into her house so silently? She knew the door was firmly shut against the afternoon heat.

"Do not be afraid, Mary. I am a messenger of God. He has sent me to tell you that you have been chosen for a very special task. You are carrying a child."

"Carrying a child?" Mary looked up in confusion and alarm. "I am not yet married – how can I be having a baby?"

The angel Gabriel moved away from the window and his light filled the room, banishing the shadows.

"He will be God's own son, a king of men and of his kingdom there will be no end. You shall call him Jesus."

"The Son of God?" Mary's hands were trembling on her lap. What would Joseph say when he found out she was carrying a baby? Would he believe the child was God's son? Would he still want to marry her? The needle slipped out of Mary's fingers and fell to the floor.

"Do not be afraid," said Gabriel. "Your cousin Elizabeth is having a child too, a son. His father Zechariah will call him John. God wants you to know that nothing is impossible for him."

Mary gasped. Elizabeth was old, well past the time when women can bear children. She and her husband, Zechariah, had been praying for a child all their married life. Now, at last, God had granted their wish.

"It is a sign that my words are true," soothed Gabriel. "Trust God, Mary. Believe in him."

Mary stood up, looking up into the angel's light. "I shall trust God. I am the Lord's servant. May everything you say come true for me."

The angel smiled and nodded. He held up his hands and a moment later he was gone, leaving behind only light reflected off the walls.

Mary pressed her hands to her belly. She was carrying a child, a boy she was to call Jesus and he was God's own son.

Married life was not going to be what she had imagined.

Jesus is Born

"I am bringing you good news of great joy for all the people: to you is born this day in the city of David a Saviour, who is the Messiah, the Lord."

LUKE 2:10–11

It had been a warm day, but now the sun had set and the air was turning cold. Joseph shivered and looked anxiously at Mary riding on the donkey by his side. What a time to be travelling! Mary's baby was due any day, any moment, really. Where would they rest for the night? What would they eat? The road they were travelling was full of people, some riding donkeys like Mary, most of them walking. A few lucky people had horses or camels with baskets of food strapped to their sides. The travellers were all going to Bethlehem, the birthplace of David, the young boy who had killed the mighty Goliath and gone on to become king of Israel. Caesar Augustus, the ruler of the whole

Roman Empire, wanted to know how many people he had in his domain. He had declared a census – everyone must register his name at the birthplace of his forefathers. Joseph was descended from David, who had come from Bethlehem, more than seventy miles away from Nazareth, where Joseph and Mary lived. So Joseph, Mary, and her unborn child had to travel all the way to Bethlehem, just to put their names down on a Roman list.

Travellers on the road nodded at Mary and smiled at the bump under her woollen robe.

"Good luck with the child! What a time to be travelling! All just to please the Romans, may God forgive them their sins."

The men turned to Joseph, nodding and grinning.

"May God grant you a son and heir."

Joseph smiled graciously, accepting the good wishes. He already knew the baby was going to be a boy. He had dreamt about a shining angel, sent by God, who had told him of it.

"Mary is going to have a child," said the angel. "A boy."

"How can that be? Mary and I are not yet married."

"Do not cast her out, even though you are not the father. The child will be the Son of God, part of God's plan for the world."

Joseph had agreed to look after Mary's son, God's son. The child was going to be his son, too. Joseph was going to look after him, watch him grow and teach him the skills he would need to make his way in the world.

"Excuse me." an old woman, plump, her hair tied up with a blue scarf, was prodding him gently. "Perhaps you ought to find shelter. Your wife…"

On the donkey, Mary was looking very tired – drawn and pale. The baby was coming. Joseph pushed his way through the crowds and knocked on the door of the first inn he saw.

"No room, sorry. We're full for the night. In fact, we're full all week. Try Benjamin's inn, down the road."

But the next inn was also full. As they went from street to street, it became clear that every inn in Bethlehem was full. There was not a bed to be had in the whole town, not even a corner of a room where the little family could lay their blankets and rest.

The last innkeeper they spoke to looked at Mary, pale and exhausted, sitting on the donkey and felt sorry for the couple. It was clear the baby was coming very soon.

"I have no room inside, but you could stay in my stable if you wish?"

"Thank you, thank you so much!"

"It's no palace, but it's warm and there's straw for you all to sleep on."

The man handed Joseph a lamp and a blanket, and pointed up a path that led behind the inn. A cow welcomed the family with gentle lowing. The stable was a cave really, made into a home for the innkeeper's animals. But after the wind-swept road it felt warm and cosy. Joseph piled up a thick mattress of hay and straw, and Mary settled onto it with a tired sigh.

Out on the hills around Bethlehem, the shepherds were guarding their flocks.

They'd had an interesting day, watching people arrive for the census. But now all the travellers were indoors, sheltering from the cold and damp. As it started to drizzle again, the hills around them echoed with silence.

Suddenly, a bright light flashed across the sky, turning the clouds a blinding gold. For a moment it looked as if the trees were on fire.

"Behold, a child is born. He is Christ the Lord."

The shepherds shielded their eyes against the dazzling brightness. In the sky was an angel of the Lord, his wings and face glowing with a mysterious light.

"Do not be afraid. I have come to give you great news. This very night, the Son of God, the Saviour, is born in the town of David."

The shepherds looked at one another. What did this mean – were they dreaming? Was it a vision?

The angel was joined by others, all singing praises to God, until the sky was teeming with winged creatures.

"You will find the Saviour in a stable, lying in a manger surrounded with straw. Go now."

The light in the sky went out. The angels disappeared, leaving the land in a deep darkness, with only the stars twinkling brighter than ever. The shepherds stood up.

"Let's go and see the Saviour, the Son of God."

They picked up their crooks, leaving a couple of lads in charge of the sheep. Then they hurried down the hill, towards Bethlehem, heading for the stable behind the inn on the traveller's road that the angel had described. They took lambs with them and food for the baby's family.

They found the Son of God on his mother's lap, his little hands curled under his chin. His father sat nearby, feeding a donkey. A cow was nuzzling the mother, keeping the baby warm with her breath.

The shepherds stopped still at the door, holding out the lambs, the food and a cloak.

"We have come to pay homage… is there anything you need?"

Joseph looked into the eyes of the shepherds and saw that they knew who Jesus was.

"Come in," said Joseph, his voice quiet but full of pride.

The shepherds crowded around the baby, their eyes wide with joy, and set their humble gifts before the mother and child.

"We saw an angel. He told us that tonight this child was born and that he is the Saviour, the Son of God."

Joseph nodded. Now he knew for sure he'd done the right thing when he decided to look after Mary and God's son. He beamed as the baby opened his eyes for a moment and wrapped his little hand around his mother's finger. God was truly amazing, Joseph realised. His son had not been born in a palace or a mansion but in a humble stable, just a cave really. And the first people to be called to the child's cradle were not nobles or princes, but ordinary shepherds – workers of the land. It was for them that the Son of God had been made human.

The Three Wise Men

They saw the child with Mary his mother;
and they knelt down and paid him homage . . . they offered
him gifts of gold, frankincense, and myrrh.

MATTHEW 2:11

Three noblemen were wending their way along the dusty road, their camels kicking up a trail of dust. They were dressed in embroidered robes of the finest cloth, their turbans and their fingers adorned with diamonds and rubies. In front of them, riding a mare, was their guide, his face wrinkled by the hot sun. Behind the noble astrologers, on horses and donkeys, came the servants, the cooks and the storytellers – a whole court, following a star that bloomed in the eastern sky many full moons ago.

People at the gates of Jerusalem stopped and stared. Visitors to the great city were often rich, powerful and impressive, but no one remembered mysterious travellers like these. None had ever seen such finery, such wealth, such wise men with so many servants carrying scrolls and charts. Where were they going? Who were they visiting?

Surely they must be guests of King Herod himself? The king was ruler

over all of Galilee and Judea on behalf of the Roman Emperor. But no, the three wise men passed the royal palace and travelled on across the great city, not even stopping to eat or rest their many animals.

A man, an official in flowing robes, came running down the street, waving a stick and shouting, "Your honours! King Herod the Great invites you to supper at his palace. Will you do him the honour of accepting?"

The three wise men had been travelling for a long time. An evening indoors was very tempting and would not hold them up for long. Perhaps this would even help them in their quest – after all, was it not a palace? It was the most obvious place for their search to end. The wise men accepted the invitation, sending word that they would be coming to Herod's palace.

"Sire," said the three, introducing themselves to the king, bowing low before his great throne. "We are Caspar of Tarsus, Melchior of Persia and Balthasar from the city of Saba in Ethiopia. We are Magi – wise men."

"Where are you heading?"

"We are seeking a king. A few months ago we noticed a bright new star in the heavens. When we consulted our charts, they indicated that a great king had been born. We have never heard of a king's coming foretold by the stars before and we wanted to see him, to pay our respects. The special star in the sky is leading us to his cradle."

A king! A new king! He might even be the Messiah! Herod laughed to mask his fear and panic. He had heard rumours too. The Jews had been waiting for someone to deliver them from the Romans and from King Herod – they knew he was really a puppet of the Roman empire.

Servants brought out a huge meal, laid out in silver bowls and served the finest wines in the land. By the end of the meal, Herod had formed a plan.

"Gentlemen, once you find this child, this new king, you must alert me at once.

I… I would like have a chance to pay my respects too."

The wise men promised. They would return to Herod with news about this amazing child as soon as they found him. The party carried on down the winding road, following their bright star out of the city, to the little town of Bethlehem. The star stopped above a little house in the hills. The wise men were amazed; they had expected a palace, at the very least a fine house. But here was the new king, in a simple house, laughing and wriggling on his mother's lap.

"His name is Jesus." Mary said, smiling and inviting the three Magi into their makeshift home.

The three wise men laid rich gifts at the child's feet; Caspar gave a small casket of gold; Melchior gave myrrh, the precious dried sap of a rare tree; finally, Balthasar set down costly frankincense. Presents fit for a king.

"We pay homage, young prince."

Their destination reached, their search over, the wise men return to their camels. What a wonderful story to tell King Herod – the new king, who was born to a humble carpenter and his young wife.

But suddenly, an angel appeared to the men, spreading his wings across the starry skies.

"Magi, do not return to Herod. He means to harm Jesus."

In his palace, the king waited impatiently. Surely the wise men should have located the child by now? They should have returned to the palace with news of his whereabouts days ago.

A messenger rushed into the room, breathless, his eyes brimming with fear.

"Sire, the wise men have gone around Jerusalem. Someone has shown them a way home through the desert."

Herod screamed with fury. Tricked! Betrayed by those Magi. Still, he would make sure the child would not grow up to steal his throne and overturn the great house of Herod. He summoned a general.

"Hurry to Bethlehem. Kill every boy under the age of two. Spare no one."

Guards streamed out into the night, their stomachs churning at the thought of what they were expected to do. Soon the streets of Bethlehem echoed with the wailing of bereaved mothers.

But Jesus, the Messiah, was not one of the innocent victims. An angel, a messenger sent by God, had woken Joseph from his sleep.

"Hurry, take Jesus to Egypt. Herod will harm him if he finds him."

Joseph roused Mary and together they packed their few belongings. He gave thanks for Caspar's gold, which would pay for their long journey. As Herod's men fanned out across the hills, seeking out every baby boy, Joseph, Mary and baby Jesus set out across the desert, towards Egypt, towards safety.

Jesus and the Teachers

After three days they found him in the temple,
sitting among the teachers, listening to them and asking
them questions. And all who heard him were amazed...

LUKE 2:46–47

A few years later, an angel of God appeared to Joseph in a dream, his wings spanning the great Egyptian night sky, his voice carried on the Nile.

"King Herod is dead. It is safe for you to take Mary and Jesus home."

Back home in Nazareth, Jesus grew into a fine boy, watching his father

planing wood, carving chests, making simple furniture. Joseph was always working, only taking time off for prayer and festivals. Mary and Joseph liked festivals. Every year in spring, they made the long journey to Jerusalem, to celebrate the Passover in the great temple, to celebrate their people's escape from slavery in Egypt so long ago.

"Can I come with you this year?" Jesus asked when he was twelve. His parents had always left Jesus behind with relatives, fearing the trip would be too tiring for him.

"Yes, Jesus, I think you are old enough to come," said Joseph. "It is time that you see Jerusalem."

Five days before the festival, the happy band of pilgrims set off from Nazareth. On the road, they were joined by pilgrims from other towns and villages, all going the same way. The caravan passed over the hills and plains, then on through the city of Beth-Shan, where both Greeks and Romans lived. The travellers stopped to admire the temples, villas and markets with goods from every corner of the Roman empire.

But soon they were passing through a huge gate, into Jerusalem itself.

"Jesus, stay close to us," warned Mary. She had forgotten how thick the crowds could be in the holy city at this time of year.

After the festival, the pilgrims from Nazareth set off for home, everyone talking about the sights they'd seen, the people they'd met. At sundown, the leader of the caravan held up his hand.

"We shall rest here for the night. Light the fires."

Mary had some lamb, Jesus's favourite, left over from the Passover meal. She would give it to him as a treat, with a chunk of bread.

"Joseph," she called, trying to spot her husband in the big throng of men walking apart from the women. "Send Jesus over for his supper."

Joseph called out from his huddle of friends. "I thought he was with you?"

"What? I assumed he was walking with the men."

Joseph hurried over, "Perhaps he is playing with the other children. They are always straggling behind."

Together, all thoughts of supper forgotten, Mary and Joseph searched for Jesus. He wasn't playing with the boys, he wasn't helping the old women make bread and he wasn't watching the guides feed the mules.

"Oh dear God, help us! Where is he?"

"The last time we saw him was in Jerusalem," one of the older boys told them. "He was running along the streets, his sandals in his hands."

"We must find him."

Joseph and Mary travelled back to Jerusalem. Going through the huge gate again, they felt as if they were swimming against a powerful current. Everyone seemed to be going the other way, out of the city. A priest helped them search the vast temple where people went to offer sacrifice. Then he sent a servant to comb the city streets with them, the inns, the marketplace.

Jesus was nowhere to be seen.

Mary drew her veil across her face. How could they have let him stray out of sight? He was only a little boy, a reckless child.

The sun was setting. The priest's servant suggested they rest in the temple courtyards. Even at night the heat in Jerusalem was unbearable. No! Mary shook her head. She would keep on searching until she found her son.

The night passed and a fierce sun rose over the city walls. Mary and Joseph continued trudging around the maze of streets, calling Jesus's name, asking passers-by if they'd seen him.

"He's tall for his age, dressed in blue – his hair needs cutting."

Many had seen a tall boy with long hair wandering around the city. But wouldn't half the boys in the country fit that description? Who could tell which one of them was Jesus from Nazareth?

On the third day, the priest's servant came running towards them down the narrow street.

"Quick! In the temple – in the corner where the scribes and teachers meet to discuss the Holy Scriptures."

They found Jesus sitting with the teachers and priests, the only one not yet old enough to have a beard. He was asking one of them a question, his chin resting on the palm on his hand.

"Jesus! Why have you treated us so? Your father and I have been looking for you all over the city."

"All over Jerusalem?" Jesus looked at his parents, amazed. "Why would you look for me all over the city? Where else would I be but in my Father's house?"

Of course! Joseph understood now. Jesus was the Son of God and the temple was God's house. Jesus had wanted to be close to his Father.

"Your son has impressed us with his knowledge," said one of the teachers. "We have never met a young man with such a deep understanding of the holy writings before. You teach him well."

Mary smiled. She was just relieved to find Jesus unharmed. But she realised that there was a lot about her son she and Joseph did not yet understand. She reached out her hand and Jesus took it. He was still just a boy, in a strange city, wanting his mother. Together they set off for home.

John the Baptist

And when Jesus had been baptised, just as he came up from the water, suddenly the heavens were opened to him and he saw the Spirit of God descending like a dove...

MATTHEW 3:16

Everyone in Judea seemed to be talking about him. The strange man who lived alone in the desert, who ate nothing but locusts and wild honey, whose only robe was a weather-worn camel pelt. Some hoped that he was the Messiah, a king who would found God's everlasting kingdom. Others insisted he would turn out to be one of the great prophets, come back from the dead to continue spreading God's message. He certainly acted like the prophets of old and spoke like them too.

From all over the country, people gathered to hear him preach, standing with his feet in the waters of the Jordan River not far from the Dead Sea.

"You must change your sinful ways," he thundered, his eyes ablaze with zeal. "The kingdom of heaven is at hand.

Just because Abraham is our ancestor does not mean the children of Israel will automatically be allowed into God's kingdom. We are like trees and be warned, every tree that does not bear fruit will be cut down."

"We repent," cried many people, wanting to start a new life following God's commands. Those that stepped forward were baptised, dunked in the shallow waters of the river as a symbol that their sins had been washed away. In the temple, some of the priests and teachers of the law heard about the Baptist and about the people who were becoming his followers.

"He will cause trouble," said one of them, in a special meeting held to discuss the matter. "The Romans do not like Jews firing up people about the Messiah – all that talk about a new kingdom on earth."

"But what can we do about him?" wondered another. "He seems to be a holy man, a prophet. Certainly his message to the people is a good one."

"Some say he is the prophet Elijah himself," added a younger priest, a scribe. "They say he has returned from the dead."

"Nonsense," said the high priest. "The man's name is John. He certainly isn't Elijah returned from the dead – his parents were the priest Zechariah and his wife Elizabeth. They died when he

was a child and he has been living in the desert ever since."

He rose from his seat. "Let us send some priests to talk to the man, to find out who he is and what he wants. Then we can deal with him accordingly."

Fired up with anger, some of the priests hurried out of the city to the banks of the Jordan where John the Baptist was speaking. A huge crowd had gathered around him – the priests had only ever seen such crowds at Passover, when people from all over the country came to Jerusalem to celebrate.

"Who are you?" called out one of the priests when John had stopped talking. "Are you the Messiah? Are you the prophet Elijah?"

"I am the voice of one crying in the wilderness," replied John, "But one who is more powerful than me is coming soon. I baptise with water but he will cleanse with fire and the Holy Spirit. Be ready for him! Repent."

The priests were furious. How dare a simple man in a camel skin tell them to repent? They pushed their way though the crowds, eager to get back to Jerusalem and the temple. It looked as if a storm was coming.

John looked at the people around him. "Those of you who wish to start a new life, to have their sins washed away, come forward. Be baptised."

Men and women, young and old,

stepped into the shallows of the river, one by one.

"I am sorry for my sins. I want to be made clean."

They stood before John, closed their mouths as John immersed them in the cold, fast-flowing water.

"I want to be made clean."

John looked up from the water to see a man standing in front of him. A man in a white robe. It was his cousin, Jesus of Nazareth. They had never met before, but John knew who he was at once. The true Messiah! This was the Lamb of God, the one who would take away the sins of the world.

"Why do you ask me to baptise you? You should be baptising me."

"Baptise me, John."

Placing his hands on Jesus's shoulders, the Baptist pushed him down gently into the muddy waters of the Jordan. Overhead, thunder rolled across the grey sky. The clouds parted, revealing a blinding light. John saw a white dove descend from the skies. It was a symbol – a symbol of God, of the Holy Spirit.

"This is my beloved Son, with whom I am well pleased."

Jesus rose from the water. He too had seen the vision, heard God's voice. Now Jesus knew his time had come. It was time to tell the people about God. He would show God's love and power as he healed the sick and helped the poor. It was time for Jesus's ministry to begin.

As John had predicted, the Messiah had arrived.

Jesus in the Desert

"One does not live by bread alone, but by every word that comes from the mouth of God."

MATTHEW 4:4

Jesus was nearly ready to start sharing God's message with the people. But first he had to do something important. Before Moses led the people out of Egypt, he had spent many days alone in the dessert with God. Now it was time for Jesus to make his own journey, alone, fasting, praying, preparing himself for the job ahead.

He went out to the desert, a wild place full of enormous, towering rocks and wind-swept valleys where wild animals hunted. Hunger gnawed at his stomach, the sun beat down mercilessly on his face and arms but he did not give in. For forty days he ate nothing, drank only the water he could scoop up in his hands from small streams and slept only when he couldn't keep his eyes open any more. All the time he prayed to God, his Father.

"Give me guidance, Lord. Let me do your will."

At the end of the forty days, weak with hunger, his skin blistered with desert heat, he was ready to return to Galilee and start his work.

"Jesus."

A man was sitting on a boulder some distance away with his back to Jesus.

"Yes?"

"You are so hungry. If you are the Son of God, why don't you turn one of these stones into bread?"

Jesus hesitated for a moment. Who was this man, could he be a shepherd? There were no sheep out here in the desert, only snakes hiding from the intense heat in crevices under boulders.

"You can do anything, you know that. And bread is so good…"

Jesus thought of the bread his mother made. He could almost smell the fresh loaf as it sat cooling near the fire.

"Man does not live by bread alone," he whispered, pushing the temptation out of his mind. He would not be here much longer – soon his fasting period would be over. The man turned his head and stared at Jesus, his eyes

burning with anger. Who was this stranger who knew so much?

Jesus closed his eyes. When he opened them again, he was sitting on top of the wall around the temple. The streets of Jerusalem were spread out below him. How had he got there? Was he really there or was he having a nightmare, brought on by lack of food? It made him dizzy just to look down.

"You are weak, exhausted," whispered the stranger. "Let yourself fall. Angels will come to help you. They will catch you in their arms before you hit the ground. You are the Son of God, after all, aren't you?"

Then Jesus knew who the mysterious stranger was. He was the devil, come to tempt him, to weaken his resolve.

"It is written," said Jesus, "that you shall not tempt the Lord your God."

The stranger snarled and a sudden gust of wind blew sand in Jesus's eyes.

"Look at the world below you, Jesus. It is all mine, it was given to me."

Jesus rubbed the sand from his face and looked. He was lying high on a cliff now, his back resting against a gnarled olive tree. He could see cities far below him, all huddled close to each other in the gathering dusk. Birds wheeled over temples. People moved around the streets, small as fleas, shopping, talking, playing.

"I would give you all their wealth, all their splendour, power over every person who lives in these lands, if you bow down before me. If you worship me."

Jesus struggled to his feet, anger showing on his face. "It is written that you should worship the Lord your God and only him. Be gone, Satan. I shall not do your bidding."

The stranger's eyes glowed with rage, with hatred. Then he was gone. Jesus felt a cool breeze on his face. Angels were gathering around him with clean water for his face and legs, a freshly washed robe and bowls of food. Jesus's time of temptation in the desert was over. He was ready to start his work among the people.

Water into Wine

Jesus did this, the first of his signs,
in Cana of Galilee, and revealed his glory;
and his disciples believed in him.

JOHN 2:11

When he left the desert, Jesus went to hear John the Baptist preach again. John pointed to Jesus and said to his followers, "Here is the Lamb of God."

One of John's disciples, Andrew, was intrigued by Jesus. He decided to follow him and learn from him. Andrew was a fisherman from the town of Bethsaida, who shared a boat with his brother, Simon.

"Why would you follow him?" Simon asked. Andrew decided to bring Simon along, to meet Jesus and hear his message.

"We are following the Messiah."

That next day another man joined the group. His name was Philip, and he too was a fisherman, from Bethsaida on the shores of Lake Galilee. He had heard Jesus speak, and like Simon and Andrew he wanted to know more about his message. Now Philip had a friend, Nathanael, who was always talking about the Messiah and how he would be coming to save the Jews.

"The Messiah is here already. His name is Jesus of Nazareth," said Philip. "I have met him."

"Don't be a fool," laughed Nathanael. "Nothing good ever came out of Nazareth, Philip."

"Come and see him for yourself," suggested his friend. "Hear what he has to say. We will pass along this road tomorrow at noon. Wait for us here and I'll introduce you."

The next day, wearing his cleanest robe, Nathanael waited under a fig tree. When he saw Philip and Jesus coming, he hurried towards them.

"Here is a good Israelite," said Jesus. "Welcome, Nathanael."

Nathanael was impressed. "How did you know who I was?"

"I knew who you were the moment I saw you under the fig tree," Jesus answered.

Nathanael grabbed Jesus's hands and pressed his lips to them.

"Rabbi, truly you are the King of Israel! The Son of God!"

"You are impressed because I spotted you under the fig tree," said Jesus. "You will see greater things yet."

The band of fishermen continued on their way. Jesus had found his first true friends and disciples.

Some days later they reached the small village of Cana, where one of Jesus's relatives was getting married. The groom's family welcomed the travellers into their home and offered them clean water to wash their hands and feet. Mary, Jesus's mother, was there already, having travelled from Nazareth with friends. She pulled her son behind a curtain, into a small storeroom.

"Jesus, I'm glad you've come. There is a problem. The family have already run out of wine. If the guests notice, the couple will die of shame."

"Mother. It's not yet time…"

"Help them, Jesus, I beg you. There are three more days of celebrations still to come. The family will become the laughing stock of Cana if they can't serve wine."

Jesus pushed the curtain aside.

"Fill those with fresh water," he instructed the servants, pointing to six enormous water jars. "Fill them right up to the brim."

Women and children rushed to do his bidding. The clay jars, each one as big as a wine-merchant's barrel, had once been filled with perfumed water for the guests.

Now that everyone had washed their hands and feet, they were empty. The servants filled them up.

"Now fill a cup for the father of the bride," said Jesus.

One of the servants fetched a goblet and dipped it reluctantly in one of the jars. Did Jesus really want the father of the bride to drink water they'd just fetched from the well outside? What was the point?

Nathanael and the disciples watched as the bride's father raised the silver goblet to his lips, drank… and smiled.

"This… this is very good wine," he gasped. "I don't understand. Most people serve the best wine first, to impress their guests. Then they serve the second-rate wine later on, because everyone is too merry to care about its quality."

He sent the servants to fill everyone's goblets. The bride and groom, the panic gone from their faces, smiled at Jesus and nodded a thank-you. Mary nodded too. Her son had saved the day. Before the wedding was

over, word had spread around Cana that Jesus had worked a miracle, changing water into wine.

Nathanael never doubted Jesus after that. Philip was right – Jesus was the Messiah after all, the one they had been waiting for. His words to his first disciples had started to come true already; you will see greater things yet!

Jesus and the Disciples

"Do not be afraid; from now on you will be catching people."
When they had brought their boats to shore,
they left everything and followed him.

LUKE 5:10–11

News of Jesus's miracles swept across Galilee and the neighbouring regions. His messages of hope and peace, of repentance and salvation in God, connected with the rich and poor alike. People flocked to hear him speak in their hundreds. Followers gathered around him, eager to learn and to help. Soon the crowds were so large, Jesus could not speak in synagogues any more. Instead, he preached out in the fields, the valleys and on the hillsides.

One day, preaching on the shores of Lake Galilee, Jesus saw two empty boats. The first belonged to Simon and Andrew's family, the second to James and John, two of those who had stayed with Jesus to hear his teachings. Simon and Andrew were nearby, cleaning their nets.

"Sit in our boat, Jesus," said Simon, "then the crowds won't hem you in."

Jesus got in the little fishing boat and Simon and Andrew rowed out a little way into the open water. Jesus addressed the crowd standing at the prow, his voice carrying on the morning breeze. When he'd finished speaking and the crowd had begun to disperse, eager to get out of the hot sun, Jesus turned to Simon.

"My friend, row further out. Let's catch some fish."

"We have been fishing all night, master," said Simon, "but we caught nothing. Still, if you want us to try again, we shall do so." He and his brother threw their net into the water, facing the wind so that it spread out as it fell.

"I can feel it filling," gasped Andrew, his muscles starting to bulge at the effort.

"Already?" Simon tugged at his end of the net. It was heavy. He started hauling the net in frantically, gasping with the effort, the rope biting into his hand. "It must be a great catch."

The net surfaced, full of jumping,

squirming, jewel-like fish. Jesus had worked another miracle.

"James! John!" Andrew called out to the other disciples near the shore. They rowed out quickly, their trained eyes noticing the churning, choppy water where the catch was. They helped to fill every basket on Andrew and Simon's boat and every basket on their own. There was enough to feed a whole village, a multitude.

"I was wrong to doubt you master," said Simon, his voice choked with regret. "I am a sinful man."

Jesus just smiled. He signalled to Andrew to take them to the shore.

"My friends, it is time to leave your fishing nets behind. From now on you shall catch people instead of fish."

Simon pulled the boat ashore, making it fast to a metal ring in the ground. Jesus was right, they wouldn't have time to catch fish any more. From now on, he and his brother, John and James and the other disciples would devote all their time to helping Jesus with his mission. They would be fishermen of souls.

Jesus the Healer

"Which is easier, to say...
'Your sins are forgiven,' or to say,
'Stand up and take your mat and walk'?"

MARK 2:10–11

One day, after coming back from the other side of Lake Galilee, Jesus was preaching inside a house in Capernaum. The room was packed with people, sitting on the floor or leaning against the rough walls. The disciples were sitting at Jesus's feet, rapt with attention. At the back were a few of the religious leaders from the local synagogues and even a Pharisee from the temple in Jerusalem. These learned men felt threatened by this popular new rabbi, this teacher who taught a message so different from the accepted Jewish laws. They were there to find fault with his teachings and to discover if his miracles were really tricks, designed to fool the gullible.

As Jesus spoke, there was a commotion at the back of the room. Four young men had arrived, carrying another man on a sleeping mat. They were trying to get close to Jesus, so that he might heal their friend. He was paralysed, unable to move at all.

"Be quiet back there, you're disturbing the rabbi."

The men pointed to the lad on the sleeping mat. "Can't you see the state this man is in? We need to get inside."

People in the crowd shook their head. "There isn't enough room in here for a mouse, let alone four big lads like you and your friend in the bed."

The four men retreated, muttering, as the crowd turned back to Jesus. The scribes smiled at one another. Would the four men interrupt Jesus again? Or would they give up and walk back up the street, grumbling that they had been turned away from Jesus, their friend still paralysed?

A strange sound interrupted the teaching again. Someone was up on the flat roof, scraping away at the mud and plaster that held the wooden rafters.

Suddenly a shaft of sunlight appeared right above Jesus. A head looked down at them, framed by the cornflower-blue sky, followed by three more. The four young men had made a hole in the roof.

"Rabbi!" one of them called.

As the crowd watched in astonishment,

Jesus looked up at the four men, squinting in the bright sunlight. Their faith in him touched his heart. He looked down at their friend, lying on the simple bed, his eyes filled with hope. "Take heart. Your sins are forgiven."

There was hissing at the back of the

the four men gently lowered their friend down into the crammed room. They had borrowed some rope from a neighbour and tied it carefully around his sleeping mat.

room. The religious leaders were muttering to each other.

"Blasphemy! No one has the power to forgive sins but God himself."

Jesus, who hadn't heard what they

were saying, read their thoughts.

"My learned friends, what is the easier thing to do: Tell a man his sins are forgiven or tell him to stand up and walk?"

The religious leaders did not answer.

"I said his sins are forgiven so that you may know I have the power and the authority from God to do both."

And he looked down at the paralysed man and said, "Rise. Take your bed and go home."

There was a moment of silence, then slowly he swung his legs off the mat. Placing the palms of his hands on either side, the man stood up. Slowly at first, he tested the strength of his feet. When he was sure he could stand, he lifted his head to his friends on the roof.

"I am healed. I can move. See?"

He knelt in front of Jesus, pressed his hands to his lips. "Thank you, master. Thank you."

The crowd, hushed by the miracle, made way for him, his sleeping mat rolled up and slung over one shoulder. The Pharisees

and religious leaders, furious at being challenged in public, slipped out of the house. Up on the roof, the man's friends started to dance, thanking Jesus for his kindness and his charity.

"Glory be to God," said the people in the crowd, "for he has given this ordinary man the authority to heal and forgive sin."

They did not yet know that Jesus was the Son of God.

Breaking the Rules

Then Jesus said to them, "I ask you, is it lawful to do good or to do harm on the sabbath, to save life or to destroy it?"... But they were filled with fury.

LUKE 6:9–11

Jesus and his disciples were walking through the fields. It was the Sabbath, the day of rest and prayer.

"What a fantastic harvest we have been blessed with this year. Every field is almost bursting with grain," said the disciple Thomas.

He picked some ears of grain and crushed them between the palms of his hands. Jesus and his disciples had been walking for a long time and all were hungry. Thomas started to eat some of the grain he held.

"It tastes good too."

The rest of Jesus's followers started picking more grain, crushing them and eating them as they walked.

"Mmmm… it is good."

Some Pharisees and other religious leaders had been following Jesus, eager to find fault with him and his teachings. Hungry travellers could always eat some of the harvest, but this was different.

"Look," they said to Jesus, "your disciples are breaking the law. They are reaping grain, but it is forbidden to work on the holy Sabbath."

Jesus answered without hesitation, "Have you not read of what King David did when he was hungry? He went into the house of God and took the bread offered to God. He and his men ate that bread, even though it was against the law to do so."

He looked at the people gathered around him.

"It is kindness that I am looking for. I am not interested in those who are cruel and hard, living their lives strictly clinging on to the law. Do not condemn people who are not guilty."

The Pharisees muttered angrily amongst themselves. Who was this man to question their teaching in front of the people? Who gave him the authority to ignore the ancient traditions, the old

Perhaps they could gather more evidence against this Jesus, something that would prove that he was just a heretic. Some of the Pharisees were worried that Jesus would lead the people away from God, but most were really just worried that they would lose the respect of the people.

As Jesus entered the synagogue, a man huddled on the floor struggled to hold out a paralysed hand.

"Jesus, help me!"

"Healing is work," muttered one of the religious leaders. "Even doctors are forbidden to help people on the Sabbath."

"Stand up, my friend," said Jesus, helping the man up. It was as if he had heard what all the Pharisees at the far end of the synagogue were whispering, though that was impossible.

"What if one of you has a sheep and it falls into a pit on the Sabbath?" asked Jesus, turning to the crowd. "Would you just sit and watch your sheep as it struggles, or would you climb down into the hole to rescue it as soon as you could? And a man is worth much more than a sheep, a humble animal. So then,

laws that they had obeyed for years? Did he not realise that if everyone started flouting the rules of their faith, evil would take over the world?

They agreed this man was dangerous.

On a Sabbath soon afterwards, the Pharisees followed the ever-growing crowds to a nearby synagogue. Jesus was meant to be teaching there and the people were eager to hear him speak.

our law must allow us to give help to those who need it, even on the Sabbath."

He turned his back on the Pharisees and smiled at the man seeking his help.

"Stretch out your arm."

Slowly, the man held out his hand and his fingers twitched and moved. He stared at his arm in wonder. He was healed!

A gasp went through the crowds. Here was undeniable proof that Jesus was no heretic. The Pharisees marched angrily out of the synagogue. They had seen enough. If word of this miracle worker spread, he could upset the whole religious community, ruin their status in the eyes of the people and undermine their power.

"We must take steps to get rid of him," hissed one of the Pharisees.

The others nodded their agreement. Yes, this Jesus was definitely a threat. From that moment they began plotting to destroy him.

Matthew the Tax Collector

*As Jesus was walking along, he saw a man called
Matthew sitting at the tax booth; and he said to him,
"Follow me." And he got up and followed him.*

MATTHEW 9:9

On the busiest street in Capernaum stood a building known as the custom house. All travellers going into and out of the town had to stop there, to show the Romans what goods they were bringing in and what produce they were taking out. They were charged taxes on everything they carried, heavy taxes that most could not afford to pay. Some of the money went to King Herod, but most of the money went straight into the coffers of Rome, to pay for foreign wars and to fund the emperor's lavish parties. But not all money collected found its way to the Romans. It was quite well known that many of the Jewish tax collectors charged more than was necessary, more than the authorities demanded. They kept the extra loot for themselves, to line their pockets.

One day Jesus was passing by this infamous custom house on his way home and he stopped to look inside.

"What is your name?" he asked one of the tax collectors.

"I am Matthew, from the tribe of Levi."

"Put down your coins, Matthew," said Jesus. "Follow me."

Matthew stood up, astounded.

"But I am a sinner. Every Jew despises me: I take the hard-earned money of my own people and give it to my Roman masters."

"Follow me, Matthew."

The tax collector put down the coins he had been counting and fetched his cloak. He had long known in his heart that the money he earned did not make him happy. He had always suspected there was something better in life than working for the Romans – something that would make him richer in another way. Perhaps he had wanted to follow Jesus ever since he had heard of him, and now Jesus had come to fetch him.

"Will you dine with me at my house tonight, master?"

"I'd be glad to," said Jesus.

Matthew's house, a fine building right in the middle of town, close to the centurion's villa, was full of people. Most of them were tax collectors, like Matthew, and other sinners, all of them despised outcasts. These people were only interested in riches, power, and all kinds of pleasures.

Jesus and his disciples were offered perfumed water to wash their hands before the meal and honeyed wine in golden cups. They had a grand feast, the best food Matthew could offer: roasted meat and vegetables, and succulent grapes, pomegranates and figs.

"Why do you sup with tax collectors and sinners?" hissed two Pharisees as Jesus left Matthew's house. "Have you no shame? You call yourself a rabbi – a teacher!"

"Those who are well have no need of a doctor," Jesus replied. "I have not come to call the righteous but the sinners, the fallen."

The Pharisees laughed cynically, but Jesus just waited patiently in the street. Eventually Matthew came out of his house, a bundle on his back.

"Follow me," said Jesus, walking towards the house where he was staying. Matthew followed, no longer a tax collector, he had become pupil of this amazing rabbi, one of Jesus's chosen. From now on he would dedicate his whole life to his new master. Jesus smiled quietly to himself. He had now found his twelve special disciples.

The Sermon on the Mount

"But I say to you that listen, love your enemies, do good to those who hate you, bless those who curse you, pray for those who abuse you."

LUKE 6:27

Vast crowds of people had gathered to hear Jesus speak. They came from all over the country, from the villages and the towns of Galilee and Judea, from Jerusalem and from the ten Greek cities called the Decapolis. They sat on the grass, their children around them, their faces turned expectantly towards one man. There were sick people among them, there were people with deformities. They had all heard that Jesus could work miracles; healed the blind, the sick. They hoped he would do something similar for them.

Jesus stood half way up a hill, so that all could see him. His disciples sat close to him, hushed, quiet. They knew their master had something important to say.

"Blessed are the poor," proclaimed Jesus, "because they will inherit the kingdom of heaven.

"Blessed too are those who are hungry; they shall be satisfied.

"Blessed are the sad, because they will find true happiness.

"And fortunate are those with a pure heart – they will meet God in heaven."

Jesus looked at the people around him, so eager to learn, to live a better life even though the odds were stacked against them.

"Blessed are those who look for peace, who reject violence. They shall be called the sons of God.

"And blessed are those who suffer for their faith, who are tortured for their choice to follow my teachings, to obey God. Their reward in heaven shall be great indeed."

A shocked murmur went through the crowd. Was Jesus expecting them to suffer for believing in him? Did they not have enough to deal with as it was, with the Roman taxes taking every penny they earned, with the grinding poverty they had to endure, the back-breaking work they had to do. Not to mention the pain and fear they felt when they fell ill…?

"You are the light of the world," continued Jesus. "Your faith makes you shine like beacons in the night. Your good deeds make you as difficult to hide as a city on a hill. So let everyone see your light, that they too might find their way to the truth."

"I bring you new laws," said Jesus. "It is written in the Ten Commandments that you should not kill, but I say you should not even hate or be angry with your family, your friends, not even with people who hate you. Forgive your

enemies everything they do to you. The Law says 'an eye for an eye, a tooth for tooth.' I say to you: embrace your enemies. When they express hatred, give them only love in return. When they try to hurt you, be kind to them instead. Do not judge people – you cannot possibly understand what is going on in their heart."

The crowd were buzzing – they had never heard anything like this before. Jesus looked at the faces turned up to his in wonder.

"When you go to worship at the temple," he said, "do not pray to God loudly with fancy words because you want others to admire you. After all, God knows everything you are going to say before you have even opened your mouth."

"How shall we pray, then, Master?" asked one of his disciples.

Jesus smiled and answered, "Pray like this,

Our Father in heaven,
May your name be honoured.
Your kingdom come.
Your will be done
On earth as it is in heaven.
Give us this day our daily bread.
And forgive us our debts,
As we also have forgiven our debtors;
And lead us not into temptation,
But deliver us from evil.

"You see, if you forgive people, then God will forgive you your mistakes. But if you do not forgive your enemies, God cannot forgive you. It is not the people who pray the loudest in the temple who get to heaven but those of you who obey God's laws because you love him.

"Anyone who follows my words will be like the man who builds his house on solid rock: neither storms nor gales will blow their faith away. But those who hear my words and ignore them will be like the man who builds his house on sand. No matter how much time he spends building a strong house, it only takes one flood, one terrible storm, and all his efforts will be swept away. It is only the true followers, those who love God, who will build their lives on my words."

A ripple of excitement went through the vast crowd. Many of those who had heard Jesus for the first time were astonished. This man did not speak like an ordinary rabbi, or religious teacher. He spoke with authority, as if he had communed with God himself. As if he was God himself.

Jesus's words rang true in their hearts. He had shown them a new way to love God and live a good life. They would follow his teachings and change the way they lived. They would be the light of the world…

The Roman Centurion and his Servant

*"Lord, I am not worthy to have you
come under my roof; but only speak the word,
and my servant will be healed."*

MATTHEW 8:8

In the town of Capernaum, near Lake Galilee, lived a Roman centurion. Capernaum was a busy town. Its streets were full of Arab traders, Jewish fishermen and Roman soldiers who worked in the military outpost beyond the fishermen's dwellings. And it had a custom house, where officials taxed the local people to swell the Roman emperor's coffers.

The centurion had recently been promoted and his wage increased. He should have been celebrating, enjoying life and making great plans for the future. Instead he was sick with anxiety because something troubled him greatly. His most trusted servant had been taken ill and was lying paralysed in bed. The centurion loved the servant as if he was his own family, his own blood. He relied on him. What would he do, how would he manage his morning that Jesus had healed a leper just by touching his hand.

He'd done it close by, on the very outskirts of Capernaum, where he and his disciples were staying. If the centurion could only talk to him, beg him, the miracle-worker might heal his trusted servant too.

"Master, Jesus is returning home. Hurry – you might catch him before he enters his house by the lake."

The centurion put on his helmet, hurried along the street after his messenger. He wanted to run, to elbow his way through the crowds, but he knew that a Roman official could never be seen panicking, sweating and flustered.

"Master."

The famous miracle worker turned and looked at the centurion standing before him.

"My beloved servant lies dying, beyond the skills of the doctors. Heal him, I beg you."

"Where do you live?"

"In the main square, next to the synagogue." the centurion smiled sadly. "But I am the enemy, the oppressor of the Jews. And I'm a sinner too. I don't

household, if the old servant died? The centurion had sent for doctors, healers, even magicians. All to no avail. His servant was getting the best care money could buy, lying under a mountain of expensive blankets, but still he was losing his battle with death.

There was only one ray of hope. The centurion had heard of a rabbi, a religious teacher called Jesus. It was said he worked miracles, healed the sick and cast demons out of the possessed. Why, messengers had brought news only this deserve to have a holy man like you under my roof…"

The centurion looked down at his hands, clenched together. Then he looked up at Jesus, trying to hold back his tears of desperation.

"But I know your powers are infinite. You do not have to come to my house. Just say the word here, in the street, and my servant will be healed."

Jesus smiled. "I tell you, not even among my own people have I encountered such faith," he raised his voice so that his disciples and the crowds around him could hear. "This man is a Roman, he bows down to Roman gods, and yet his belief in me is complete."

He turned to the centurion. "Return home. Let it be done as you have believed."

The Roman centurion nodded and followed his messenger back home. Hastening up the path to the door, his heart pounding with effort and hope, he could hear servants running, shrieking. The front door burst open.

His cook stood on the doorstep, tears running down her cheeks.

"Master, your servant is well. Not a moment ago, he opened his eyes! I gave him a cup of broth to stave his thirst. It is a miracle!"

Beyond the wall of his villa, the Roman centurion could hear the crowd following Jesus towards the Lake of Galilee. Some of the Jews called this man their anointed one, their Messiah-king. Perhaps, thought the centurion, Jesus had brought hope not only for the Jews, but for the entire world…

Jesus the Storyteller

"But as for that in the good soil, these are the ones who, when they hear the word, hold it fast in an honest and good heart, and bear fruit with patient endurance."

LUKE 8:15

"Tell us a story, Master. Tell us one of your tales."

"Yes, a story, Teacher. A story."

Jesus, sitting on a boat, spoke to the people around him. He used parables often because the crowds were used to hearing stories and fables. They told them round the fire at home, or while watching the sheep, or working in the fields. Storytellers were popular people, often called to courts of kings or to rich men's houses to entertain. But Jesus's stories were not mere entertainment. He told them for a purpose. It was not obvious at the time, but when people thought about his stories and repeated them to friends, they began to think about God's love, how they wanted to live and how they should treat each other. Jesus looked around him at the eager faces and began…

"One hot day, a farmer was sowing seeds – scooping them out of his bag with one hand and scattering them around as he walked. Some seeds fell on the stony path and the birds swooped down and ate up those seeds. Some fell in shallow soil, among rocks. At first little shoots sprang up, but those seeds could grow no roots and their tiny bit of soil held no water, so they withered away. Other seeds fell into the thorns. The thorns grew much faster than the sprouting seeds and eventually they choked the little shoots. But some seeds fell on good, fertile ground. The seeds grew into strong, golden wheat and gave the farmer a great harvest."

"What does that story mean, Master?" asked one of the disciples.

"The seeds are the people who hear about God's kingdom," said Jesus. "Sometimes the word falls on deaf ears; the people don't understand what they hear. They turn away and the message is lost. Those people are like the seeds that fall on the stony path.

Some people take the word of God to their heart, but when things get tough, they give up. Those people are the seeds that fall on shallow soil.

Some, after hearing the word of God, cannot act upon it. Things happen in their lives, or their friends and families might persuade them not to follow my teachings. After a while, the message is lost. Those people are like the seeds that fall into the thorns.

But some people, like the seeds that fell on fertile ground, accept God's message and live their lives according to it."

"That is a wonderful story!" said the disciples and the people around them. "Please, Jesus, tell us one more."

"There was once a rich merchant who dealt in pearls," recounted Jesus, "buying and selling them at the market. One day, a traveller showed him a prize specimen. It was the finest, the most perfect pearl the merchant had ever seen, as bright as the full moon on a clear night.

The merchant knew he would never be happy, would never sleep again, until he possessed that wondrous pearl. He auctioned all his other treasures, he sold his house, he even bartered his clothes until he had enough money to buy the pearl. Only then was he at peace.

The pearl is like God's kingdom. It is worth more than everything else in the world put together."

Then the people understood what Jesus was trying to tell them, and they went away eager to retell all of Jesus's stories to their families and friends.

Jesus Calms the Storm

*And they were filled with great awe
and said to one another, "Who then is this,
that even the wind and the sea obey him?"*

MARK 4:41

The crowds around Jesus were getting bigger by the day, the hour. Men and women, children and grandparents, rich and poor, they all wanted to see this man everyone was talking about, to be touched by his words. Some of the Pharisees and teachers of the Law were getting more concerned about Jesus's popularity. Who could control all of these people, these hysterics? Even the Roman officials were beginning to take notice and were asking why they could not keep this man under control and why weren't they ordering the people to go back to their villages.

"Jesus is becoming a problem," admitted the priests. "He teaches and yet he was not trained for the priesthood. He knows the Holy writings, but he elaborates on them as if he had written them himself."

On the shores of Lake Galilee, Jesus had been teaching the crowds by using parables, short stories with spiritual meanings. He felt the crowds understood his messages better that way, even his disciples. But now he was tired and weak from hunger.

"Let us go to the other side of Lake Galilee," he said. "It'll be quieter there."

Simon fetched his boat and Jesus climbed in. He went to sleep right away, resting his head on a cushion at the stern, the back of the boat. It was a still evening, the sun setting behind distant clouds. Not a breeze ruffled the calm water.

Andrew and Simon lit a lamp to show their friends the way. It was getting dark and other disciples were following, rowing their boats across the lake where they once fished.

Suddenly, without warning, the wind rose up, blowing out the lamp. The sun had set and it was pitch dark, the moon

hidden by clouds. Above the disciples' heads, the rolled-up sail knocked against the mast, threatening to fall. It started to rain.

"Master! Master, wake up!"

At the stern, Jesus went on sleeping, the pillow under his head. The wind turned into a gale, tossing the boat up and down as if it were a nutshell or the cork from a wineskin, bobbing on the waves. The rain turned into a deluge, soaking their clothes in seconds, pouring into the fish baskets, filling up the water jars, even the boat itself.

The disciples were terrified. The boat would surely sink, it could not withstand the storm, and they would drown! They grabbed water jars and started to bail out water as fast as they could, but it was useless. The boat was sinking.

"Master! Master! Wake up – we are going to drown!"

Simon shook Jesus awake. He sat up and looked around at the raging storm. Water seemed to pour in from all sides and the boat was rocking wildly now and the disciples had abandoned their water jars.

"Be still," Jesus called into the wind. "Be calm," he ordered the waves.

In an instant, the wind dropped and the sea was like glass. A full moon slid out from behind the clouds, turning the lake to silver. The disciples turned to Jesus in silent wonder; the only sound the dripping of water from their robes.

Jesus turned to his disciples, "Did you think I would let you die? What little faith you have…"

The disciples said nothing, but started bailing water again. Now that it had stopped raining they would be dry in no time at all in the fierce heat of the night.

Amazed, the men asked one another, "Who is this man that the forces of nature obey his orders?"

Healing the Little Girl

"If I only touch his cloak, I will be made well."
Jesus turned, and seeing her he said, "Take heart,
daughter; your faith has made you well."

MATTHEW 9:21–22

Jesus was getting out of Simon's boat and beginning the walk to his home, when he was approached by a man dressed in fine linen robes and wearing costly jewellery.

"Teacher, my daughter…"

The man threw himself at Jesus's feet, his hands pressed tightly together, his expensive linen and gold necklace trailing in the dirt.

The disciples could tell at once who he was. This was Jairus, one of the leaders of the synagogue in Capernum. Was it not his friends who were always frowning at them as they entered the synagogue and shaking their heads to show they did not approve of their master's teachings?

"My daughter is dying. She is only twelve. I saw you heal the man with the withered hand in the synagogue and I thought if only you would come to my house and lay your hands on her…"

Now it was the disciples' turn to frown. How could this man humble himself in front of Jesus? To ask for a miracle when all of his friends at the synagogue would only shake their head as Jesus spoke! Surely Jesus would turn down his request, send him back to the synagogue to teach the other leaders a lesson about their behaviour?

"Where do you live, Jairus?"

"On the main street."

To their astonishment, the disciples saw Jesus following Jairus.

"Jesus! Jesus!"

As they passed the fish market, people recognised the healer, the miracle-worker, and a crowd formed around him. Everyone wanted to see Jesus, to speak to him and to be blessed by him.

"Someone touched me," said Jesus. He stopped walking, looked around him.

"We're always surrounded by people,"

"Your faith has indeed healed you. Go in peace."

The master's words were drowned out by several men rushing down the street. They were beating their hands with their hands, sobbing and wailing.

"Sir, your daughter has just died. She has breathed her last."

They were servants from Jairus's house on the main street. Jairus gasped; his hands flew to the neck of his robe, ready to tear it apart as a sign of mourning.

"She is not dead," Jesus said. "Do not fear, only believe."

He beckoned Simon, James and John to follow him and they hurried through the crowds, up the main street to Jairus's house.

"Why are you weeping?" said Jesus to the mourners who were already assembled in the yard, ash smeared on their faces. "This girl is not dead, she is only sleeping."

"She is dead. We held a veil up to her lips and it did not move. She drew no breath."

Jesus asked everyone to leave the house – the servants, the relatives, the curious neighbours. He took Jairus and his wife by the hand, called the three disciples, and they entered a small room where the child was lying on her bed, her face pale, her eyes shut.

Jesus took her little hand in his. "Talitha, koum. Little girl, arise."

said Simon. "It's no wonder somebody touched you, Master."

"This was a different touch," said Jesus. "Someone touched me with faith, with their belief. They kissed the hem of my robe."

A woman stepped out of the crowd, trembling. Like Jairus, she threw herself at Jesus's feet.

"It was I, Master. I have been sick for a long time, I am unclean and for twelve years I have been bleeding. No doctor could cure me. But I knew that if I as much as touched the hem of your robe, I would be well again."

Jesus bent down and helped the woman to her feet.

The girl's eyes fluttered open. She gasped and breath passed her lips.

"Mother? Father?"

"Your parents are here," smiled Jesus. "Sit up."

The girl obeyed him, throwing off the blanket the servants had wrapped around her. Jairus and his wife stepped forward and hugged their daughter tightly.

"What's the matter, Father. Why are you crying?"

"Your parents are very happy to see you." said Jesus. "I believe the girl is hungry, get her some food."

He washed his hands in a basin.

"Tell no one about this, Jairus. Those who heard of it would then come to me for the wrong reasons, they would not understand that it was done through your own faith."

"Yes, Master."

Jesus ruffled the girl's hair, smiled. Then he was gone, eager to get home, to rest. The disciples followed him, silent, thoughtful. Jesus had just helped a rich man who worshipped at the synagogue where they did not approve of him, did not follow him. And he had helped a poor, unclean woman. Truly his love reached out to one and all.

The Death of John the Baptist

For John had been telling Herod, "It is not lawful for you to have your brother's wife." And Herodias had a grudge against him, and wanted to kill him.

MARK 6:18–19

It wasn't right, commoners telling royalty what to do, working men interfering in the private life of their king. Like John the Baptist, a man who lived in a cave, who wore nothing more than an animal skin wrapped round his unwashed body. He had the cheek to shout at King Herod, ruler of Galilee and Perea and son of Herod the Great! And on the way to the temple too, when so many people were gathered, all with God on their mind.

"King Herod, it is not right for you to be married to your brother Philip's wife, even if she is pretty and clever. You are already married, you already have a wife."

Herodias, the new wife, the dazzling queen, had felt as if she would die of shame. All those people staring at her, all those scribes and priests snickering behind their hands. In her heart she had sworn revenge on the Baptist even as the king's personal guard had grabbed him and bundled him off.

Her husband, though, was afraid of the Baptist.

"We cannot have him executed," Herod had said when she broached the subject. "The people trust and respect the Baptist. If we harm him, his disciples might whip them up into a frenzy. It would not look good for me if they attempted an uprising. My position with the Romans is fragile enough as it is. I couldn't cope with any trouble."

Fear of the Romans was not the only reason Herod was reluctant to kill the Baptist. Herodias knew there was a bigger fear gnawing at the king's heart. He secretly believed that John was right: he should not have taken Herodias as his wife. The fool seemed to admire the Baptist, he seemed to respect him as much as the common man in the field did. The king could not help listening to his words, even though he became greatly disturbed every time the holy man opened his mouth.

Herodias had nagged and coaxed and argued until the king gave in. Although, being such a thick-headed fool, he only agreed to the first part of her request.

John could not insult her in public any more, but now there were even more of his followers on her trail. They made her life a misery, shouting at her when she left the palace, echoing their leader's warning.

"Repent, you sinner!"

"Obey the laws of God. No man or woman who lives in sin should rule over our people!"

Herodias realised she would have to

Herod had the Baptist arrested, but not killed, not silenced forever. Instead he had the prophet put behind bars in a remote fortress overlooking the Dead Sea. The man who had once explored the desert at will, who had slept under the stars every night, was now confined to a cell, his legs in chains.

Much good that did Queen Herodias!

get rid of the Baptist herself. Then perhaps his demented followers would find someone else to harass, another message to shout and a new leader to follow. Her chance came on her husband's birthday. A great crowd assembled in the palace for the birthday feast. Roman officials and military commanders, wealthy merchants,

leading pillars of the community; all came bearing gifts and messages of goodwill for Herod.

The king called for his wife's beautiful daughter, Salome.

"Entertain us, my child."

The girl was a talented dancer. To the sound of bells and tambourines, she whirled gracefully around the great hall, shedding veils from her face until all assembled were stunned by her talent and beauty.

"She is a most enchanting creature," cried the members of the audience, stamping their feet and holding up their chalices.

"She is indeed a rare gem," agreed Herod's distinguished friends.

Herod, carried away by his guests' enthusiasm, spoke up in a loud voice, "That was truly beautiful. Ask for whatever you want, my child, and I will grant it."

Herodias, leaning forward on her throne, whispered something in her daughter's ear. The girl paused and then turned to the king.

"Sire," she said. "Above all things, I would like the head of John the Baptist brought to me on a silver platter."

A gasp escaped the crowd in the room. Herod turned deathly pale.

"My child…"

"You said I could have anything I want, Father."

The king was trapped. How could he refuse, in front of so many important guests? His reputation would not survive the evening.

"Guards," he bellowed. "Go to the prison. Do as the girl asks."

Some time later, Salome entered Herodias' chambers with a servant following her, carrying a silver dish.

"For you, my mother."

Even as the queen looked at the severed head, disgust fighting triumph in her cold heart, servants had slipped out of the palace, spreading the news.

"The Baptist is dead. John the Baptist is dead."

When news reached Jesus that his cousin was dead, he wept silent tears.

Five Loaves and Two Fishes

Jesus said to them, "They need not go away;
you give them something to eat." They replied,
"We have nothing here but five loaves and two fish."

MATTHEW 14:16–17

Early one morning Jesus gathered twelve of his friends around him. There was Simon, his brother Andrew and the brothers James and John. These men had all been simple fishermen but had left this work to become Jesus's first disciples. There was Philip, also a fisherman; another James, the son of a man called Alphaeus; Bartholomew, also known as Nathanael; Thomas; the second Simon; Thaddeus; Judas Iscariot and Matthew the tax collector. These were his special disciples, the twelve men who would teach on his behalf, who would spread his message among the people.

"Go out and preach in my name. Tell people to repent from their sins. Heal the sick, cast out demons. Take nothing with you except a staff to help you walk. Carry no food, no extra clothing, no money in your belts. If people are kind to you, stay in their house, preach to them. But if anyone turns you away, don't even take away the dust from their doorstep with you. Brush it out of your sandals to show they have not accepted the Lord."

Nodding in agreement, the men set out in pairs to do as Jesus had told them. Many of the people who heard the twelve chosen disciples speak then searched out Jesus so that the crowds around him grew bigger by the day. When the disciples returned to Jesus, he suggested they cross Lake Galilee in a boat, to escape the crowds.

"You need to rest," he said, "come away to somewhere more remote."

But when the boat reached the other side of the lake, the crowds were already there, waiting for Jesus. They had heard he was coming and now cries rang out as they spied the boat on the water.

"Tell us a story, Master."

"Heal my father, Master, I beg you!"

Jesus took pity on the crowds – they seemed to him like a flock of sheep without a shepherd. He healed the sick, he preached, he told parables.

The sun was beginning to set, a great golden ball setting the whole sky on fire. One of the disciples spoke to Jesus.

"It is getting late, Master. You must send these people home."

"This place is too remote," answered Jesus. "There is nowhere to buy food, no inns where they can stop to eat. We cannot send them home hungry."

"But Master, we do not have any food to give them."

Jesus asked the disciples to see what food they could find. Only one young boy had anything to eat; he had just five small loaves and two fishes.

"That is not enough for us, let alone this crowd," said one of the disciples. "There are more than five thousand people here."

"Divide the crowd into groups," instructed Jesus. "Tell them to sit in hundreds and fifties. No one will leave here hungry."

The disciples looked doubtfully at Jesus, but did as he asked them. Jesus took the loaves and the fishes and looked up at the heavens.

"Bless this food, Father."

He broke the loaves and handed them to the disciples with the fish.

"Give them out," he said. "Turn away no one."

The disciples carried the food to the people, breaking each of the loaves into smaller pieces.

"Here you are. Take some fish and some bread."

The food should have run out before they had been around the first group, the first gathering of fifty, but it didn't. The disciples kept on moving through the crowd, handing out bread and fish. By the time the sun had set, the entire five thousand had eaten their fill. Now people were shaking their heads, refusing any more helpings.

"No, truly, I cannot eat any more."

The leftovers filled twelve enormous baskets. The people were astounded, amazed. Everything they'd heard from the disciples about Jesus seemed to be true. He was indeed a very special man, perhaps the Messiah himself.

The people began to leave, blessing Jesus's name.

Jesus Walks on Water

*He intended to pass them by. But when they saw
him walking on the lake, they thought it was a ghost and
cried out; for they all saw him and were terrified.*

MARK 6:48–50

While the crowds were dispersing, their talk only of the great miracle they had just witnessed, Jesus called the disciples together.

"Go and get the boat ready."

"Master, are we leaving now?" asked the disciple Simon.

"I am going up into the hills, alone, to pray for a while. Take the boat across the lake to the west bank."

The disciples got in the boat, taking the remains of the loaves and fish with them. They would give them to the poor and hungry on the other side of the lake.

The sun set and a sudden wind blew across the lake. The disciples unfurled the sail and soon it had caught the gentle breeze that would carry them to the far bank.

Simon wondered where Jesus was and what he was doing. Soon, darkness fell. The wind grew stronger by the minute and suddenly changed direction. Water sprayed the disciples' faces, blinding them. Before they knew it, the disciples were out in the middle of the lake. Some of them struggled to keep control of the oars, while others rushed to furl up the sail and tie it to the cross beam.

This was a dangerous time of year, when sudden storms churned the waters of Lake Galilee, dashing helpless vessels against the rocks. For many hours they rowed against the wind and asked themselves whether they would ever see Jesus again.

"Look, brothers."

Thaddeus was pointing to a lonely figure on the water. It seemed to be floating above the waves.

"It's a ghost."

"A dead man walking!"

The figure got closer, its face blurred by rain and spray.

"Do not fear. It is me."

Simon tried to wipe the water from his eyes. "Jesus?"

"Have heart. I will not let you drown."

Simon's mind was reeling. First Jesus feeds five thousand people with five loaves of bread and two fish and now he walks on water. Was he really there, calling out to them, or had they lost their minds in the terrible gale?

"Master," he cried. "If it is really you out there, call me to you. Let me walk on water too."

Jesus held out a hand. "Come."

The other disciples looked on amazed, as Simon swung one leg over the side of the boat. He put a foot down on the water – it did not sink. He swung another foot over, his hands gripping the side.

Holding his breath, Simon took one step away from the boat, away from its safety. The world went silent around him. He, Simon the simple fisherman, was walking on water. Walking towards Jesus.

But then a stinging wave splashed Simon's face, and for a moment he lost sight of Jesus. A cold voice whispered deep inside him. "This is not happening. You are only dreaming."

Wiping the water from his eyes, ignoring the voice, Simon focused on Jesus's outstretched hand.

"Come, Simon."

Step by step, he approached the master, reaching out his hands. But the voice of doubt whispered to him again.

"Foolish man. What are you doing? You could drown!"

Suddenly Simon's feet plunged through the waves; freezing water stung his eyes. The voice in his head had been right – he was sinking.

"Master, help me!"

Jesus's hand reached through the water. "Oh man of little faith! Why did you doubt?"

In a moment he was walking again, side by side with Jesus, across water as smooth as glass. Philip and Matthew helped them both back into the boat.

The wind dropped as quickly as it had begun, leaving the disciples to unfurl the sail again and continue their journey.

"Shall we set sail for Bethsaida, Master?" asked Philip.

"To Bethsaida," confirmed Jesus. "We need some rest."

But none of the disciples slept that night. As the sun rose, all they could think of was this latest wonder.

"Truly," they said to each other, "this man is the Son of God."

Who is this Man?

"Get behind me, Satan!
You are a stumbling-block to me; for you are setting
your mind not on divine things but on human things."

MATTHEW 16:23

Jesus and his disciples were close to the pagan city of Caesarea Philippi, the capital of Herod Philip's kingdom. As they got nearer to the worship site, people thronged around them: pilgrims and merchants, travellers seeking work, children begging for alms. When they reached the famous cliff, where the sheer rock marked the place of worship, the noise was deafening and the heat of the sun was searing on their skin.

"Who do these people say I am?" Jesus asked his disciples.

The men looked at one another, not quite knowing how to answer. It was an intriguing question. Who was Jesus, really? Everyone knew he was the son of Joseph the carpenter, brought up in Nazareth. They knew his mother was Mary and that he did marvellous things. He preached to thousands, he walked on water, he healed the afflicted and the sick. But, who was he? What was he?

"Some say you are John the Baptist come back to us from the dead," ventured Matthew.

"Some say you are the prophet Elijah," added Andrew.

"Or another prophet," interrupted Mark. "A few have claimed you are the great prophet Jeremiah."

"But you, my disciples," said Jesus, stopping in the shade of a tree, "who do you say I am?"

The answer leapt straight out of Simon's mouth. "You are the Christ – the Son of the living God."

The others stared at him in astonishment. Simon was easily the loudest, most outspoken of them all. He was always the first with questions, the quickest to argue and the one most likely to make a fool of himself. Where had those words come from?

"Bless you, Simon, son of John," replied Jesus. "Flesh and blood has not revealed this to you. It has been revealed to you by my Father who is in heaven. From now on you shall be called Peter, which means 'rock'. You shall be the foundation of my ministry, my church. I shall give you the keys to the kingdom of heaven, and whatever you bind on earth will be bound in heaven but that which you loose on earth shall be loosed in heaven."

Jesus looked from one disciple to the next, each face full of surprise and awe.

"I beg you not to tell anyone that I am the Messiah, for it is not yet the time for my suffering. I warn you now, when the time comes I shall go to Jerusalem and there the priests and scribes will reject me and my teachings. I shall be tortured and killed. On the third day after my death, I will be raised to life again by my Father and the scriptures will be fulfilled."

Peter could not stand to hear that his master would face such suffering.

"God forbid, Lord. I hope these terrible things shall never happen to you."

"No!" said Jesus, suddenly angered. "That is Satan speaking through you Peter. Don't you see that he distracts you with human concerns to make you forget God's intentions?"

Calm again, Jesus turned to speak to the other disciples.

"If any man wishes to be my true disciple, he must deny himself, take up his cross and follow me. For whoever tries to save his own life will lose it, and whoever offers his life in my name will find everlasting life in heaven."

The disciples looked at each other, as they realised the power of what Jesus was saying.

"What would a man gain," said Jesus quietly, "if he owns the whole world yet loses eternal life? My friends, if you are ashamed of me and of what I say, I shall be ashamed of you when I return in the glory of my Father. I promise you this; some of you here today will not taste death before you see the Son of Man coming in glory with his kingdom."

Jesus and the Children

"Whoever becomes humble like this child is the greatest in the kingdom of heaven. Whoever welcomes one such child in my name welcomes me."

MATTHEW 18:4–5

The disciples were crowded around a well on the outskirts of a dusty town, their throats parched, their sore feet covered in sand. Children swooped in and out of the group, full of energy, like hungry swallows looking for food. They reminded the disciples of something that Jesus had said a few days before.

"Jesus," James had called. "Will you settle a question for us? Who is the greatest in the kingdom of heaven?"

Jesus had looked from one man to another. He knew his followers had begun to understand that they had been chosen to take part in something great, something vital to God's plan for his people. And they all wanted to be an important part of it; they all wanted to be someone special.

He called a child to his side.

"Truly," he said, smiling down at the little one, "unless you become like a child, you will never even enter the kingdom of heaven."

The disciples exchanged puzzled glances – what was Jesus saying? That they had to start playing with toys again or climbing trees to look for birds' nests?

"You must be as innocent as a child," Jesus had pointed out. "Whoever humbles himself like this child, he is the greatest in the kingdom of heaven."

It was then that the disciples began to understand: it wasn't the man who worshipped the loudest or the man who impressed and entertained the crowds who would prove to be Jesus's most treasured disciple. It would be the person who served God faithfully, without any thought of praise, or glory, or financial gain.

Women started gathering around the well. The sun was going down and they had come to fill their jars with water. One of them poured water into the disciples' cupped hands, splashing it on to their dusty feet.

"Drink, cool yourselves. You must have walked miles today."

A mother with a baby on one arm and an older boy clinging to her skirt, looked up from her water jar.

"Jesus, bless my children – I beg you."

Matthew scowled and spoke for all the other disciples. "We have walked far today and the master is tired. Come back tomorrow."

As if he had not heard Matthew's words, Jesus smiled at the mother, touching the hair of the infant in her arms. The older boy grinned and moved forward shyly, hoping that the miracle-worker would touch him in blessing too. A second mother came up, pushing her children forward. She was soon joined by an old grandmother with a newborn baby wrapped in the folds of her cloak and a slave leading a rich scribe's daughter.

"Bless our children, Jesus."

"Lay your hands on the little ones."

"Take pity, Jesus – this poor mite has walked with a limp ever since he fell out of an almond tree."

All of a sudden, the disciples were surrounded by women, begging and pleading to have their child blessed. Peter jumped to his feet and started pushing them away roughly.

"Can't you see the master is tired? He has been preaching all day; he has cured the sick, healed the blind and blessed many, many people. Now he needs to rest. If he blesses your children the whole village will come out, wanting to blessed or healed. Come back in the morning, I tell you."

"Let the children come, Peter," said Jesus sharply. "Do you not understand? These are the pure in heart. They have faith in me without doubt and trust me without question. They do not seek power or glory or money, for they are the humble, the meek."

And he swept the children into his arms, hugging them close. At that moment the disciples remembered Jesus's words about becoming as humble as the children.

"The kingdom of heaven belongs to children such as these."

The Rich Young Man

Then Jesus looked around and said . . .
"Children, how hard it is to enter the kingdom of God! . . .
[but with] God all things are possible."

MARK 10:23–27

The crowds around Jesus parted to let through a rich young man, the son of a respected man in the local community. He approached Jesus with a smile on his handsome face, his brand new sandals squeaking on his perfumed feet, the diamonds in his many rings catching the light of the sun. The young man's friends had told him all about Jesus and his message and he wanted to learn more.

"Master, what must I do so that God will grant me eternal life?" he asked, kneeling on the dusty road.

"Obey the commandments," replied Jesus. "Honour your father and your mother; love your neighbour as you love yourself; do not kill or steal; and do not tell lies."

The young man smiled. How easy it seemed for an educated, well brought-up man to act correctly and be granted eternal life.

"Master," he said confidently, "My parents brought me up to follow the holy commandments."

"But there is another thing you must do," said Jesus. "If you want to be truly perfect, go and sell everything you have, all your treasures and possessions, all your comforts. Donate all the money you have to the sick and the poor – that way you will have your treasure in heaven, rather than hoarding it here on earth, where everything turns to dust. When you have done all this, come and follow me."

When he heard this, the rich young man rose shakily to his feet. This was not the answer he had been expecting.

"But, Master," he protested, "my parents would be ashamed of me if I were to become a penniless wanderer – they have their position in society to uphold. How can I give away everything I own – my fine hand-carved furniture, my costly jewels, my large flocks of sheep and geese? I could not possibly part with my beautiful robes or my beloved, ancient scrolls. Why, my family has worked day and night to earn such riches. It is all no less than we deserve."

With those words, the rich young man backed away into the crowds, shaking his head sadly, and was gone.

Jesus turned to his disciples.

"I tell you truly," he declared, "it is easier for a camel to pass through the eye of a needle than for a rich man to enter the kingdom of God."

The disciples stared at one another in consternation.

"Who can possibly be saved, then?" asked Matthew.

"What is impossible for man," Jesus assured them, "is always possible with the help of God."

"That's true," cried Peter. "Haven't we given up everything we have to follow you, Jesus? Surely that means we, at least, deserve to enter the kingdom of God?"

Jesus answered him in a quiet voice, "I say to you, Peter, that anyone who has left his house and everyone he knows, his parents, brothers, sisters and children; he who has abandoned his land or his boat in my name, shall receive back a hundred times what he has lost. He shall gain eternal life."

Then he looked carefully from one disciple to another.

"But remember, those who work only to gain a reward in heaven shall be the last to receive it, while those who expect nothing for their good deeds shall be first in the eyes of the Lord."

The Tax Collector

All who saw it began to grumble and said,
"He has gone to be the guest of one who is a sinner."

LUKE 19:7

Jesus, the great teacher, the one who worked miracles, was travelling near Jericho. Someone had seen him with his disciples, approaching the city along the banks of the Jordan and had run to the city to spread the news.

The streets were full of excited people talking, jostling for position and craning their necks to catch a glimpse of this famous man. Was Jesus on his way to Jerusalem for the great feast? Would he stop in ancient Jericho, the city of palms, whose mighty walls had fallen at the sound of God's trumpets, so long ago?

Among the crowds was a man called Zacchaeus. His fine robes and expensive jewellery were those of a rich and important man – the chief tax collector in the city. But as Zacchaeus walked through the crowd, people turned their back on him and ignored his greetings. Tax collectors were popular with the Romans – the rich, foreign invaders who occupied their country – but here on the street, Zacchaeus was regarded

as no better than a greedy worm, stuffing his coffers at the expense of his neighbours. A man like that had no right to even glimpse this great teacher.

A murmur of excitement swept through the crowds. Jesus had left the high road, was coming through the city gates. Many started running, the infirm crying out for help, the blind holding their hands out for protection. Zacchaeus started running too. He had heard a lot about this Jesus and he wanted to see him, to be part of the great story, if only for a brief moment.

The crowds surged around him like an angry sea, threatening to drown him. Zacchaeus was very short, not much taller than a boy, and so he could only see a wall of tunics and shawls. How would he be able to catch a glimpse of Jesus with all these people towering above him? The tax collector looked around. He needed a vantage point, somewhere high up that would give him a good view of the road.

There was an old sycamore tree right next to the city gate, its long branches arching over the main street of Jericho. Zacchaeus elbowed, squirmed and fought his way through the heaving sea of people. When he reached the old sycamore tree, Zacchaeus started grappling his way up it, the rough bark giving him good purchase.

"Hey, little man, what do you think you are doing?" shouted someone in the crowd below.

"Why, it's Zaccheus, the chief tax collector!" shouted another man, unable to hide his amazement at seeing the vain and greedy tax collector shinning up the tree like a common street urchin.

The crowd started to jeer.

"Your servants kicked you out of your own litter, have they, Zacchaeus?"

"Repenting our sins, are we, tax collector? You'll be here all night!"

A carpenter who had two children clinging to his waist, started shaking his fist at Zacchaeus.

"What makes you think Jesus would forgive the sins of a traitor like you? Go back to your expensive home and hide behind your wooden shutters. Jesus of Nazareth has come to get rid of people like you, not to bless them."

The crowd roared its agreement with the carpenter. Zacchaeus closed his eyes. The crowd sounded so angry – were they going to pull him down from the tree and beat him?

A sudden hush fell on the crowd. Zacchaeus opened his eyes and saw a man standing under the tree, looking up at him. His eyes were different from the other eyes in the crowd – instead of empty hatred they were full of kindness.

"Zacchaeus, come down!"

How did this man know his name? He must be the teacher, Jesus!

"I must stay at your house tonight, Zacchaeus. Come down and show me the way."

Zacchaeus nearly fell out of the tree, his surprise was so great. Jesus wanted to come to his house, a house built on money taken from the poor, every brick bought with the suffering of his people.

Zacchaeus scrambled down the tree, not caring that his new robe was getting torn and dirty.

"You are welcome, my Lord." said Zacchaeus and suddenly he was overcome with emotion.

The crowd parted to let Jesus and Zacchaeus through.

"Jesus, Zacchaeus is a tax collector – would you be a guest in the house of a sinner?" roared the carpenter, his face red with anger, his two children hiding their faces in his tunic.

Jesus looked into the tax collector's eyes. At any moment Zacchaeus expected to see the disgust there that he so richly deserved, but Jesus simply smiled at him.

"Prepare food, sweep out the best room in the house!" shouted Zacchaeus to his servants. "We have honoured guests tonight – Jesus and his disciples shall sup with us."

As they turned towards his house, Zacchaeus burst out, "I shall give half of everything I have to the poor. Oh Lord, if I have ever cheated anyone, I will pay them back four times over…"

Jesus smiled, "Salvation has come to Zacchaeus' house today, for he too is one of God's children. The Son of Man came to seek and save the lost."

Martha and Mary

But the Lord answered her,
"Martha, Martha, you are worried and distracted by
many things; there is need of only one thing."

LUKE 10:41–42

"The teacher is here! The teacher is here! He and his disciples have come. Welcome, welcome Jesus. We are blessed to have you in our humble home again."

Jesus had close friends who lived in the small village of Bethany on the outskirts of the holy city of Jerusalem. He often stayed with a man called Lazarus and his two sisters, Mary and Martha. The family was rich and respected, owning beautiful vineyards and giving work to many of the people of Bethany.

Martha rushed to spread out mats, to tidy their home and sweep the courtyard. She hurried to fetch the best food in the house: freshly baked bread, olives steeped in the finest oil, wine straight from the merchant's house, salted fish.

Mary did not offer to help her sister. She wanted to hear every word Jesus said, to commit it to memory. He was unlike any teacher Mary had ever heard. Jesus dared to criticize the priests in the temple and he pointed out the good in those who were frowned on by everyone else. What he said seemed to ring true in Mary's heart, to say the things she had not even realised that she felt.

Mary and a few of the disciples sat in the shady courtyard, listening to Jesus as he told them stories and answered questions. Martha, hot and sweating from all her hard work, glowered as she brought out the food and poured their best wine into cups.

"Mary, I need you to help me. I am sure our guests are hungry."

Her sister didn't hear her. She was too absorbed by Jesus's words.

Martha spoke a little louder. "Mary, if you could give me a hand with these heavy jars…"

Once more Mary took no notice. Slamming down a heavy jar, Martha could not hide her anger any longer.

"Jesus," said Martha in an angry tone. "Do you not care that my sister has left me to serve alone? That she is sitting here with you while I am working so hard? It is not right. You must tell her to help me."

Jesus had stopped his story when Martha interrupted him. Now, to her amazement, Jesus seemed to side with Mary.

"Martha, Martha, you are distracted by trivial things – worried about matters that are not important. There is just one thing that

is important for you now, just one thing that you really need to do. Mary has chosen rightly – she pays attention only to what is essential. Now, Martha, put down your work and sit with us."

Finally Martha stopped worrying about feeding her guests, cleaning the house and making everyone comfortable. Instead she joined her sister at Jesus's feet, finally ready to listen to his every word.

Healing the Lepers

One of them, when he saw that he was healed,
turned back, praising God with a loud voice.
He prostrated himself at Jesus' feet and thanked him.

LUKE 17:15–16

"Unclean! We are unclean. Keep away, we are unclean."

The disciples could hear them long before they rounded the bend: a group of men, their faces hidden behind rags and dirty bandages, walking slowly and painfully along the main road to the great city of Samaria.

The disciples around Jesus shivered. Each of the men had a terrible skin disease: such things could be caught by touching a sufferer's hand, maybe even just by breathing the same air.

"Keep away! Unclean! Unclean!"

Jesus stopped in the middle of the road. There was a village nearby but the men, ten of them as far as the disciples could see, could not have come from there. Those with terrible diseases were not allowed to live anywhere near the healthy folk. They usually found sanctuary in caves or deep gorges far from the prying eyes of local people and the taunts of their children. The priests allowed them into the synagogue but they had to stay away from the rest of the faithful, a sign that they had done something to anger God.

The ten men threw themselves to the ground, "Jesus of Nazareth, we have been told that you can heal the sick. Please, have mercy on us."

Jesus's quiet reply carried down the road on the afternoon breeze.

"Go and show yourselves to the priests in the synagogue."

Go to the priests? The men struggled to their feet, new hope giving them strength. The priests were the ones who could pronounce them healed, the ones who could declare them fit to join society again.

One of the men looked at his arm. The round white marks, the sign of the loathed sickness, were disappearing in front of his eyes.

"Look, brothers!"

Amazed, the others pulled up their sleeves and tore the rags from their faces.

"The scales are falling from our arms – our skin is clearing!"

"Let's hurry to the priests!" shouted the oldest among them, the one they looked to for advice. "Let them tell everyone that we are clean."

"Wait," one of the ten said, looking back at the disciples through a film of tears. Jesus was standing among them, still as a statue. "Thank you."

His throat tight with emotion, the healed man had only been able to mouth the words. He wasn't sure that Jesus had heard him. As his friends hurried to the synagogue, he ran back down the road towards the disciples, feeling the strength return to his legs.

"Thank you, Jesus." He threw himself down at the teacher's feet, his voice high-pitched with joy with gratitude.

"Were not ten cleansed?" said Jesus. "Where are the other nine? Was no one found to return and give praise to God except this foreigner?"

The disciples looked at the man. Now they realised he was a Samaritan, one of those people who set themselves apart from the Jewish people, with their own scriptures and their own temples. The Jewish people reviled the Samaritans – some even claimed that they were possessed by evil spirits. Yet out of the ten men Jesus had healed, it was only the Samaritan, still on the ground at Jesus's feet, who had thought to thank their master for the miracle.

"Rise," said Jesus, helping the Samaritan to his feet. "It was your faith that healed you." The man stood up and began walking to the nearest village, thanking God and praising Jesus's name.

The Good Samaritan

"He went to him and bandaged his wounds, having poured oil and wine on them. Then he put him on his own animal, brought him to the inn, and took care of him."

LUKE 10:34

Jesus was on his way to Jerusalem. A crowd had gathered around him and Jesus was talking to them when a teacher of the Law of Moses stood up.

"Jesus, I have a question," asked the well-dressed man. "What can I do to gain eternal life?"

"What does it say you should do in the Scriptures?" replied Jesus.

"It says that you shall love the Lord your God with all your heart, with all your soul, your strength and your mind. And you must love your neighbour as much as you love yourself, too."

"Do this," said Jesus, "and you will have eternal life."

"But what do the Scriptures mean by the word 'neighbour'?" asked the man, still wanting to test Jesus. "Do they mean the people who live next door to me? Do they mean my friends? Or strangers with the same faith as mine?"

"A man was travelling from Jerusalem to Jericho," said Jesus, by way of explanation. "Walking on a lonely road, he was attacked by robbers who stole all his belongings, beat him cruelly and left the man for dead on the side of the road. Some time later, a priest came by on his way from the temple."

The people in the crowd sat forward expectantly. They knew what was going to happen next in the story – the priest would help the poor man. Priests were always good and wise men.

"The priest saw the traveller lying in the ditch and crossed to the other side of the road, so he could pretend that he had not seen him and therefore would not have to stop," said Jesus. "Not long afterwards, a second man came walking down the road: a Levite."

Everyone listening to the story knew who the Levites were, too. Long ago, in the time of Moses, God had appointed men from the tribe of Levi to look after the temple. They were not priests, but people who were dedicated to the service of God nonetheless. Surely the Levite would help the poor man?

"Thinking that this could be a trap, laid by thieves seeking to rob kind travellers, he too crossed to the other side of the road," said Jesus.

"Eventually, a Samaritan came along, riding on a donkey."

A Samaritan! The crowd knew he wouldn't help the poor man in the ditch. The Samaritans had their own temple and their own Scriptures – they considered themselves to be better than ordinary Jews and the ordinary Jews thought that they were better than the Samaritans. Thus the Samaritans and the ordinary Jews had grown to hate each other.

"The Samaritan spotted the man on the ground and stopped his donkey at once. When he realised the traveller was hurt, he poured soothing oil on his wounds and bandaged them with strips of cloth from his own robe. Then he lifted the man gently onto the donkey and took him to the nearest wayside inn.

"'Here is enough money to pay for this man's care and for his food,' he said to the innkeeper. 'I can't stay to look after him, but if you spend more than this, I shall repay you on my way home.'

"And having handed over the money, the Samaritan continued on his journey."

The crowd was silent as Jesus finished his parable. To think – a Samaritan who helped an injured man when a priest and a Levite would not.

"Which one of these three men do you think proved to be the traveller's neighbour?" Jesus asked the teacher of the Law.

The man answered without hesitation, "The one who helped him – the good Samaritan!"

"Go," said Jesus to the man, "and be a neighbour to everyone you meet. That is how you will have eternal life."

The Prodigal Son

"When he had spent everything… he went and hired himself out to one of the citizens… who sent him to his fields to feed the pigs. He would gladly have filled himself with the pods that the pigs were eating; and no one gave him anything."

LUKE 15:14–16

"Have you noticed the sort of people who gather around Jesus?" sniffed the religious leaders and the learned men in the temple. "Sinners and tax collectors – people who hobnob with Gentiles and serve the Romans. He even enters the houses of fallen women and eats at their table!"

A few days later, word reached Jesus of the way that the religious leaders disapproved of him.

"If a shepherd has one hundred sheep and loses one of them," said Jesus, preaching to a large crowd, "does he not leave the ninety-nine to search for the one that's lost? Does he not keep on searching till he finds it? And when he returns home with the missing sheep on his shoulders, he calls together all his friends, to celebrate its safe return."

Many among the crowd knew that Jesus's story was a direct challenge to the religious leaders – after all, who was more lost than fallen women and tax collectors? Looking at the expectant faces of the crowd, Jesus began to tell another parable.

"A wealthy landowner had two sons. The younger one was impulsive and headstrong. One day he came to his father and said, 'Father, give me now the money you would have left me in your will. I mean to go out into the world and enjoy myself – I don't want to wait until after you are gone.'

"The man was saddened by his son's words, but he gave him the money.

"As soon as he was given the money, the son left home and moved to a distant land where the young man quickly and

foolishly squandered his inheritance.

"With no money or possessions left, the younger son's friends soon deserted him. He wandered the streets alone, getting hungrier and more frightened until a farmer took pity on him and gave him work; he had to go out into the fields and look after the pigs. The young man was so weak with hunger, he gazed longingly at the slop meant for the animals. He had not eaten anything as nourishing in days.

"'Even my father's lowliest servant has proper bread to eat,' thought the young man. 'I shall return home and beg my father to take me back as a servant in his house.'

"Early one evening, the landowner saw his son returning home across the fields. He ran out to meet the son he thought was lost and hugged him close to his chest, tears of joy on his cheeks.

"The son fell to his knees in front of him. 'Father, I have sinned. I am not worthy to be called your son, but please take pity on me and let me be a servant in your house.'

"But the landowner would not listen to such talk – his son, whom he had given up for lost, had returned home and he wanted to celebrate.

"The wealthy landowner gave his son new clothes and a ring for his finger.

"The eldest son, returning from his work in the fields, heard music and the sound of dancing.

"'What's going on?' he asked a servant who was fetching water from the well.

"'Great news, sir! Your younger brother has returned home. There is to be a big celebration – your father has killed the fattened calf in his honour.'

"'Come, my son, join us,' called his father, coming out to the well.

"'No,' said the older son, his face twisting in anger. 'I will not join you. All these years I have worked for you and obeyed you, but you never once gave me one scrawny goat or lamb to share with my friends. Yet when my brother returns – he who has frittered

away half your fortune on sin – you kill the fattened calf meant for the festival!'

"'My son, you are always with me,' replied the landowner. 'And everything that I have is yours. Do not begrudge your brother one fattened calf. How can I not rejoice when he who we thought was dead has returned home safe, he who was lost to me has been found?'"

Jesus looked at the faces in the crowd around him.

"I tell each of you, there will be more rejoicing in heaven over one sinner who repents than over ninety-nine people who do not need repentance."

Lazarus

"Those who walk during the day do not stumble, because they see the light of this world... Our friend Lazarus has fallen asleep, but I am going to awaken him."

JOHN 11:9–11

Lazarus, the brother of Mary and Martha, was gravely ill. The sisters sent word to Jesus, who was teaching on the banks of the Jordan, far from his opponents in Jerusalem.

"Jesus, your friend Lazarus is very ill," the messenger told him breathlessly. "His sisters know your work keeps you away from them, but they beg you to return and help him."

The messenger returned to Mary and Martha with a puzzling answer.

"This illness is for a purpose," Jesus had said. "It has happened so that more people might see the glory of God and come to believe in the Son of God."

What could Jesus mean?

"It doesn't matter," sobbed Mary when the messenger returned. "We sent you too late. Lazarus died an hour after you left. We have already buried him."

"In any case," said Martha, hugging her sister, "we would not want Jesus to risk coming so close to Jerusalem; his enemies are everywhere. The Pharisees are spreading malicious rumours about him, calling him a heretic."

But a few days later, a boy ran in from the fields, trembling with excitement.

"Mistress," he whispered to Martha. "Jesus is approaching with his disciples."

"Jesus – here? I must go to meet him outside the village," Martha said. "Our house is full of mourners from Jerusalem – we can't risk someone betraying us and telling the priests he is here."

Wrapping her face in a shawl, Martha rushed out to meet Jesus. Her eyes welled with tears as she saw him coming over the crest of the hill.

"Master, Lazarus is dead. If only my messenger had reached you in time... If only you had been here..."

"Do not grieve, Martha," Jesus consoled her. "Your brother will live again. Do you not believe that?"

Martha spoke through her tears, "Jesus, I believe that all people who accept your teachings will live again on the last day, the day of resurrection."

"I am the resurrection and the life," said Jesus. "Everyone who believes in me shall live, even if they die, and those who live and believe in me shall never really die."

"You are truly the Messiah, the Son of God," said Martha, moved by his words.

By now Jesus had been spotted and a crowd of locals gathered on the streets.

"Master! Master!"

"Where is Mary?" asked Jesus.

"She's in the house. Shall I fetch her?"

But even as Martha spoke, Mary was pushing through the crowds, her eyes red and swollen with weeping and lack of sleep.

"Master, if only you had been here, our brother would have lived."

Jesus wiped away Mary's tears. He had a troubled look in his eyes that showed he was feeling the same pain as his friends. Death was so cruel…

"Where is Lazarus buried?"

"In the family tomb, Master."

The two sisters led Jesus and his disciples to an olive grove behind their house, the rest of the village and the mourners following close behind them. The entrance to the tomb was sealed with a large, round stone that Martha's servants had pushed into place.

"Remove the stone," said Jesus.

"Master," cried Mary, "he has been dead four days. There will be a stench."

"Do not fear. If you only believe in me, today you will see the glory of God."

The servants rolled away the stone away from the tomb and Jesus knelt at the entrance, facing the darkness inside.

"Father," he prayed, "I thank you for hearing me. I know that you always

listen to my requests but I am saying this aloud so that everyone gathered here will believe that you have sent me."

Then Jesus stood up and called out in a loud voice, "Lazarus, come out."

There was movement inside the cave; a white shape in the shadows. Suddenly a hand reached out from the darkness.

"Lazarus," Jesus repeated, "come out."

His friend stepped out of the shadows into the sunlight, a white veil falling from his face.

"Lord!"

"Remove the burial sheets that bind him," said Jesus. "And fetch water – my friend is thirsty."

Martha and Mary rushed to their brother, hysterical with joy, kissing his face as they tore the strips of linen from his hands and feet.

"Thank you, Master – you truly are the Son of God."

All around the grove, the crowd watched in stunned silence. Jesus had worked yet another miracle. And this time he had shown without a shadow of doubt that he was indeed the Son of God, the Messiah.

The news spread quickly from Bethany to Jerusalem – Jesus had raised his friend Lazarus from the dead. He had proved that he was the Deliverer, the Chosen One.

In the temple in Jerusalem, the chief priests and Pharisees called a special meeting. Caiaphas, the high priest that year, spoke to them, his face red and voice loud with anger.

"This man becomes more of a danger to our authority every day. It was all right when he stayed far away, in the backwaters of the north. But now the rumour is that he has raised the dead on our doorstep, under our noses! People are turning away from us to him. The Romans expect us to keep our nation under control. How can they have faith in us, if they see we can't keep one man under control? I think this Jesus must die."

All the other men in the room raised their hands in agreement.

"Jesus must die."

The King on a Donkey

"Hosanna! Blessed is the one who comes in the name of the Lord! Blessed is the coming kingdom of our ancestor David! Hosanna in the highest heaven!"

MARK 11:9–10

A young donkey stood tethered to a tree in the village square. It was nearly Passover and the road outside the village was full of people on their way to Jerusalem. It was not far to the holy city – from the donkey's home, Jerusalem's walls could be seen rising into the sky.

Snatches of conversation drifted over on the breeze.

"We are going into Jerusalem for Passover. I want to preach in the temple."

"But, Master, will it not be extremely dangerous? There will be large crowds of people from all over the country. Many have heard you teach or seen you perform miracles – some are already saying that you are the long-promised king, the Messiah. One more challenge to the authority of the religious leaders and the Sanhedrin might arrest us all."

"Matthew, what is written in the Scriptures about me will come true," answered Jesus in a calm voice.

The disciples looked at each other helplessly – they could not prevent him from going. They must follow him.

Jesus spoke to Matthew and John. "Go into the village. There you will find a young donkey tied to a tree. Bring it to me."

"But what if the owner accuses us of stealing it?" asked Matthew.

"Tell them the Lord has need of it and will send it back immediately."

Matthew and John hurried down the path into the village. The donkey's owner had heard of the famous miracle worker, the man who forgave sins, healed the sick and brought the dead back to life. He was surprised – they said that one day this Jesus would be king. Surely a king would want to ride a mighty stallion? Perhaps an impressive Arab steed with a flowing mane – something to reflect how powerful he was.

But when the disciples told him Jesus's message, he could only nod his consent. The donkey was untied from the tree and led along the path to the main road – to Jesus himself.

Someone threw a few cloaks across the donkey's back, patting them down to make a comfortable seat.

"Thank you," said Jesus, getting into the hastily-made saddle. He rubbed the donkey's head. "Come on my friend, we are going into the city."

As they approached Jerusalem, the crowd spotted Jesus and surged around them. The young donkey was unbroken – it had been tethered to the tree every day for its whole short life – but the good-natured animal was not frightened.

Pushing and jostling to get a better view, to welcome the king, people waved palm branches and threw them, along with their cloaks and blankets, onto the road. They formed a rainbow carpet into the city for the donkey to walk on.

"Look – it's Jesus from Nazareth."

"It's the miracle worker!"

"He healed my cousin – cured him with one touch!"

A deafening cheer echoed around the city, ringing against the ancient walls, sending doves flapping into the skies.

"Hosanna! Welcome to the King, the son of David himself."

"Blessed is he who comes in the name of the Lord."

"Hosanna! Hosanna!"

Had there ever been a more joyful entry into the city? With his gentle hands, Jesus guided the donkey along the streets of Jerusalem. Soon, the smell of burning sacrifices hung in the air and the chant of the people as they prayed to God could be heard. At last they approached the great temple itself.

Jesus climbed off the donkey and the crowd followed him, reaching out to touch him, calling his name. A disciple led the donkey to a nearby inn, gave him straw, rubbed down his dusty coat, heavy with sweat from his exciting journey. For a brief moment, one of the humblest of all animals had been part of the greatest, the most glorious event in history: the coming of the Messiah to save the world. For carrying Jesus on this one short journey, the donkey would be remembered forever.

The First Betrayal

"But woe to you, scribes and Pharisees, hypocrites!
For you lock people out of the kingdom of heaven.
For you do not go in yourselves,
and when others are going in, you stop them."

MATTHEW 23:13–14

The religious leaders were furious. They had tried to trick Jesus into saying something against the Romans, against Caesar – one hint of treason and he would have been clapped in irons and dragged to prison. But they had failed miserably! Jesus was too wise to be tricked by the priests and scribes. Rather than attacking the Romans, he had criticised the religious leaders themselves – the keepers of the temple who were supposed to be the leaders of the people. He had called them hypocrites and fools!

"After that fiasco in the temple, we have to get rid of him – and soon!" shouted Caiaphas, the high priest.

Following his joyous entry into Jerusalem, Jesus had headed straight for the temple. In full view of the crowds, he had overturned the money-changers' tables and released the animals and birds being sold for sacrifice. Jesus had shown to everyone that he condemned all the buying and selling that went on in the Court of the Gentiles. He was showing the people that he blamed the priests in particular because they had allowed the house of God to be turned into a common market – how could anyone pray to God amidst all this noise?

"The people on the street are finding wisdom and inspiration in his words," muttered a priest. "They find our rules too complicated to follow; his message is easier than ours."

"If only he would go somewhere far from all these crowds," hissed Annas, Caiaphas' father-in-law. "Without the protection of those crowds, we could use the temple guards to arrest him. We could tell the Romans that he was preaching treason – they would never know he has not actually said a word against them."

"We have to be careful," a scribe reminded him. "Passover might not be the right time to arrest such a popular teacher. The people might start a riot and attack the temple itself if we tried to harm him."

"The people might even revolt against the Romans themselves," said Caiaphas, "and then what would happen to us?"

As he spoke, a guard brought in a furtive-looking man, his face tanned a deep brown, his frayed robe bleached by the sun.

"I am Judas Iscariot, one of the twelve closest to Jesus."

The priests threw suspicious glances at one another. Was this some sort of trap set for them by the rebel? Caiaphas spoke for them all.

"Why do you seek us out in the temple, disciple of Jesus?"

"Only yesterday," whispered Judas. "I witnessed a woman pouring expensive balm on Jesus's head. Pure nard, it was – very costly, as you know. When I complained that it should have been sold and the money given to the poor, Jesus reproached me. 'The poor will be with you always,' he said. 'But you will not always have me.'"

"Is Jesus seeking to travel, then?" asked Annas. "To leave you all to fend for yourselves against the authorities?"

"I do not understand the master any more," said Judas. "I am scared and confused. They say that the Messiah will free us from the Romans, but Jesus does not seem to care that our people live in bondage. He only talks of his Father in heaven. Where is this all leading?"

"Perhaps we should ask Jesus these things," said a priest. "Do you know where we can find him, alone and far from the crowds?"

Judas nodded slowly, but his soul was screaming inside him. Why was he so confused? Why was he even talking to the master's enemies? He was betraying Jesus; the priests were sure to arrest the master, if they could find him. And yet, somehow, this seemed to be the right thing to do, as if he was fulfilling some strange destiny.

"Will you promise that he will not be harmed? Jesus is only doing what he believes is right."

The priests gave their assurance.

"You have our word; we shall not hurt him."

"He prays in the Garden of Gethsemane at night."

"Gethsemane?"

"On the outskirts of Jerusalem, at the foot of what is called the Mount of Olives."

Caiaphas nodded at a scribe, who thrust a bag of coins into Judas's hands.

"A gift for your assistance; thirty pieces of silver. Imagine how many poor you can feed with that."

Judas thrust the money under his robe. Yes, he could help the poor with the silver. Jesus had always insisted on helping the needy and the afflicted. Now his disciple was doing the same.

"You will lead us to Gethsemane very soon, Judas," said Caiaphas. "But how will we know which of the men is Jesus of Nazareth? Even with the guards' torches, the garden will be very dark ."

"You will not make a mistake. I shall point him out to you," insisted Judas.

"And how will you do that?"

"With a kiss. I will walk up to Jesus and kiss him on the cheek."

The Last Supper

"...the one who betrays me is with me, and his hand is on the table. For the Son of Man is going as it has been determined, but woe to that one by whom he is betrayed!"

LUKE 22:21–22

Passover, the largest, most important festival of the Jewish year, was about to begin; a festival that would last a whole week.

"Where shall we have our special Passover meal tonight?" Peter and John asked Jesus. They were just outside Jerusalem, in the countryside where many pilgrims camped during Passover.

"Go into the city," replied Jesus. "A man carrying a water jug will meet you. Follow him and, when he enters a house, knock on the door yourselves and speak to his master. Say to him: the teacher asks where he is to eat the Passover with his disciples? That man will tell you."

The disciples carried out Jesus's instructions

and were shown into an airy room at the top of a house. They spread mats on the floor and prepared lamb, unleavened bread, bitter herbs and wine – each food a symbol that would remind the guests of the night their ancestors followed Moses out of Egypt. The disciples did not know that tonight would be a special night too, a night that would eventually be celebrated by millions of people all over the world.

Late in the evening, Jesus arrived with the other disciples. He poured water into a basin.

"Come – Peter, James, everyone. Let me wash your feet."

Peter looked startled – bathing feet was the most lowly servant's job. Why would his teacher, his great friend and master, insist on doing it? Jesus saw the question in Peter's eyes as he began to wash the dirt of the road from his disciples' feet.

"You must serve one another as I have served you today," said Jesus. "Truly, I say to you, a master is not greater than his servant."

At last, Jesus dried his hands and took his place at a low table on which the food had been laid in bowls and the wine poured.

"Even as we sit here," Jesus said, "one of you is working to betray me."

The disciples looked at one another, horrified. Who would dare betray Jesus, and how? Could there be a traitor among them, someone who in some way would sabotage their Master's work?

"Master, who will betray you?" said John, who was sitting right next to Jesus.

"He who I give this bread to," said Jesus, and he dipped his bread in one of the dishes, and handed it to Judas Iscariot. "Go," he said. "Do what you have to, quickly."

And Judas rose, his face flushed with anger, and left the room. The remaining disciples heard the door slam shut behind him, his feet clattering down the street outside. What was Judas planning to do? He was in charge of the group's money – had he stolen it and given it to the temple? They couldn't understand.

Jesus picked up more bread, blessed it and passed it round.

"Take, eat; this is my body."

He lifted a cup of wine.

"Drink. This is my blood, which is shed so that all sins might be forgiven. My blood will mark God's new agreement with his people. I tell you, I shall not taste the fruit of the vine again until I drink it in my Father's kingdom, in heaven."

"Why not, Master?" asked one of the disciples.

"I will be going somewhere that you cannot yet follow, my friends," answered Jesus, "but do not be troubled. I shall be with you always. Love one another as I have loved you, and share wine and bread in remembrance of me."

As I have loved you! Jesus had spoken to them of his own death before, but now he seemed to be speaking as if his life was going to end very soon, as if some terrible catastrophe was just about to happen.

Was Jesus really going to leave his disciples, his loved ones?

In the Garden of Gethsemane

He came and found them sleeping; and he said...
"Could you not keep awake one hour? Keep awake and
pray that you may not come into the time of trial;
the spirit indeed is willing, but the flesh is weak."

MARK 14:37–38

"Let us go to the foot of the Mount of Olives," said Jesus as they finished the Passover meal. "I want to pray."

They walked along the streets out of the city, some of the disciples keeping an eye out for temple guards.

"Tonight," Jesus said, "you will all abandon me. For it is said that when the shepherd is gone, the sheep will scatter. But when I return from my long journey, I shall go before you to Galilee."

Peter, walking close to Jesus, held his breath. Their leader was talking about leaving his disciples again. Where was he going, and when?

"Even if everyone else deserts you," he said, "I shall remain faithful."

Jesus looked at him sadly, "Peter, even before the cock crows in the morning, you shall have denied me three times."

"Never," cried Peter. "I would gladly lay down my life for you, Master. You know that."

The men reached the Garden of Gethsemane and most of them sat by the entrance, hiding in the shadows, keeping watch. Jesus chose three of them – Peter, James and John – to walk with him further into the grove. The disciples could tell that Jesus was really troubled; that he was expecting some event to happen quite soon. Surely nothing horrible could occur tonight of all nights, when all those of the Jewish faith should be celebrating freedom?

"Wait here and keep watch for me," said Jesus. Then he left them and moved further in among the trees.

"Father," Jesus whispered, throwing himself on the ground. "Take this cup of suffering away from me, for I am afraid. I know everything is possible for you – you can save the world without my blood being shed. And yet you must do what you will, and not what I want."

The moon came out, revealing the three disciples who were meant to be guarding him. They had fallen asleep and were snoring peacefully. The wine had obviously made them drowsy.

"Peter, could you not watch with me for an hour?"

The disciples woke up, rubbing the sleep from their eyes. But they were too tired to stay awake for long: twice more, Jesus had to rouse them. The third time, they heard voices in the grove and saw torches smoking against the inky sky.

"My hour has come," said Jesus. "My betrayer is here."

A man stepped out of the shadows into the moonlight. It was Judas, bringing with him some of the priests and Temple guards.

"Master."

He kissed Jesus on the cheek.

Immediately, the soldiers pounced, swords drawn, chains rattling.

"You could have arrested me in the temple or on the street," said Jesus. "Instead you come for me in the dead of night as if I were a criminal. But it was written that it would happen so. Let the prophecy be fulfilled."

The chief guard tightened the irons around Jesus's wrists. Someone pushed him forward roughly.

"Do not attempt to flee."

None of the disciples stepped forward to help their master. All had run away and hidden in terror, as Jesus had told them they would, Peter with the rest.

Jesus is Condemned

...the whole council were looking for testimony against Jesus to put him to death; but they found none. For many gave false testimony against him.

MARK 14:55–56

Coming out of his hiding place, Peter followed the soldiers at a safe distance. Where were they taking Jesus – to the temple or to the Roman governor's palace?

The party passed through one of the city gates, heading to the western part of Jerusalem, where the rich priests and the noble families lived. The master was being dragged to the mansion of Caiaphas, the high priest.

To Peter's surprise, a large crowd had gathered just inside the priest's gate. Most were members of the Sanhedrin and their guards – they had obviously known Jesus would be taken that night. But there were also other people there, brought to testify against Jesus. How many, Peter wondered, had been bribed?

He slipped closer, mingling with a few curious people in the courtyard who were watching the crowd through doorways and window spaces.

The council members, gathered on the steps leading up to Caiaphas's door, filed into the house. Inside, the senior members took their seats on gilded chairs as if for a Roman spectacle. The high priest nodded to the chief guard.

"Who have you brought before us?"

"This is Jesus of Nazareth."

Caiaphas opened his arms to include the crowd in his courtyard.

"Who will testify against this criminal who would bring the wrath of Rome down on us? None of us will be safe until he is silenced, but we cannot bring him to justice until we have witnesses."

People stepped forward, eager to speak. Peter wondered, had their courage been bolstered with money – the voice of their conscience drowned out by jingling coins?

"I heard him say many times he is the Messiah. He even said it in the temple."

"I heard him too. I heard him too."

A burly man raised his hand. "I heard him say he is able to destroy the temple and rebuild it all in three days."

The high priest scowled. The claim that anyone, even the Messiah, could rebuild the temple in three days was not something to be taken seriously. But wanting to tear down the temple of Jerusalem was another matter. That could be seen as encouraging rebellion.

"Do you have nothing to say in your defence?" Caiaphas asked Jesus.

The prisoner did not even reply.

"I ask you, in the name of the living God," said Caiaphas tauntingly, "if you really are the Messiah, the Son of God, tell us. We will understand."

Jesus looked the high priest in the eye.

"You say yourself that I am," said Jesus. "And you shall see me sitting at the right hand of God, my Father."

There! They had him at last – condemned by his own words! The man had blasphemed in front of witnesses. He had claimed he was not just the Messiah, but God himself. The priests had a real reason to destroy him now, a reason that people would understand.

Before the council, Caiaphas tore his robe in two as a sign of penitence.

"The man is a blasphemer. You heard him! What should his punishment be?"

One of the elders stood up, "We do not need men in our midst who poke fun at God. There is only one punishment suitable for this crime: we propose death."

Peter's Denial

"Truly, I tell you, this day, this very night, before the cock crows twice, you will deny me three times." But [Peter] said vehemently, "Even though I must die with you, I will not deny you."

MARK 14:30–31

Death! The news spread quickly to those out in the courtyard; Jesus was going to be executed like a common criminal. Peter staggered back down the steps of Caiaphas' mansion, his mind reeling. Would the temple guards come after him and the other disciples too, once Jesus was gone?

Only a few days ago, Peter had felt so strong, so sure of what he was doing. Now he was racked with doubt again, confused and frightened – possibly even on the run for his life.

Even though the dawn had not yet arrived, the street seemed full of people. A maid carrying charcoal to a brazier bumped into Peter.

"Aren't you are a friend of Jesus?"

It was unbelievable! Peter had already been recognised, right outside the high priest's house.

"I don't know the man."

An older servant joined the maid.

"But we've often seen you walking with him or sitting at his feet when we came to hear his teachings."

Peter backed away from the burning embers into the shadows.

"You must be mistaking me for someone else, old man. I have never met Jesus of Nazareth."

"You have!" said the servant. "Why do you deny it?"

Why? The old man must know what had just happened in his master's house – didn't he realise that it had suddenly become dangerous to be known as a friend of Jesus of Nazareth? The fickle crowd was already turning against the teacher, calling for his blood! Coming stealthily in the night, the priests had proved too clever for Peter's master and they would prove to clever for the disciples, too.

"This man is a follower of Jesus," said the old servant indignantly to a friend who'd come to warm himself by the fire. "He denies it, but we know that it's true."

"It is not true," shouted Peter.

As the sun began to cast its first rays, a cockerel on top of the wall behind them crowed to announce the dawn.

Peter froze. The master had said that Peter would betray him three times before the cockerel announced the dawn – and after all his promises, all his vows of loyalty, Peter had done so without a second thought!

"Forgive me, Master," Peter whispered hoarsely and, turning from the fire, he ran out into the night.

Jesus Before Pilate

*Pilate asked him again, "Have you no answer?
See how many charges they bring against you." But Jesus
made no further reply, so that Pilate was amazed.*

MARK 15:4–5

"Governor, we have brought a dangerous criminal for judgment."

The priests, even the high priest himself, did not have the power to carry out the death sentence, so Caiaphas had brought Jesus to Pontius Pilate, the Roman governor of Judea. Only the Roman ruler could condemn a man to death – that was why the priests had taken Jesus to the Antonia, the palace of Pilate, that loomed over Jerusalem. The governor always stayed there during Passover, in case there was trouble.

"What is his crime?"

"He claims to be the king of the Jews."

The priests knew that blasphemy against the Jewish god was not a crime under Roman law. So they had changed their charge to one of treason against the Roman Empire.

"He has also told people not to pay their taxes, as an act of rebellion."

Pilate turned to Jesus.

"Are you the king of the Jews?"

Jesus replied, "You have said so."

"These are only foolish words," Pilate said to the priests. "I find no malice in this gentle man of whom I've heard. He is a rabbi who teaches people only to love your god. That is no crime – even we Romans are taught to love our gods."

"But, sire," insisted Caiaphas. "He has been preaching rebellion all the way from Galilee to Jerusalem."

"Has he?"

Pilate realised that the priests had another motive; they wanted to get rid of this man because his teachings were becoming more popular than theirs, not because he was a threat to Rome. Beneath their thin smiles, the priests hated Rome with all their hearts. How crafty of them to accuse Jesus during Passover, a volatile time when any other governor would err on the side of safety and have the suspect killed instantly.

And yet, what would happen to Pilate if Jesus did turn out to be a rebel and caused some sort of uprising? Would he be accused of bad judgment, perhaps demoted from office?

Pilate decided at once what he had to do. Every Passover, the Roman governor in Jerusalem released a prisoner of the people's choice – let the people decide if Jesus should go free. He would pit this gentle teacher against an unpopular criminal. If anything happened later, the governor could tell them that he had released Jesus against his will, because of the tradition.

The govenor sent guards to fetch one of the most repulsive prisoners.

"Which of these men will you free for Passover?" Pilate asked the crowd. "Jesus of Nazareth or the infamous Barabbas, murderer and rebel?"

"Free Barabbas!"

"Barabbas! Release Barabbas!"

Pilate stood before the masses, stunned to silence by their decision. This was no ordinary crowd – it must have been bribed by the temple scribes, its anger roused by the mention of blasphemy.

"People of Jerusalem, what shall I do with Jesus of Nazareth?"

"Give him what he deserves!"

"Crucify him!"

"Put him to death!"

Furious that he had been tricked by the priests, Pilate called for a basin of water.

"I am merely having the condemned man flogged. The death is all your doing," he snapped at the priests. "I wash my hands of this sorry spectacle."

Death on a Cross

"...and darkness came over the whole land until three in the afternoon, while the sun's light failed; and the curtain of the temple was torn in two."

LUKE 23:44–45

The Roman soldiers, still waiting for their orders, were having fun taunting Jesus.

"Hail, King of the Jews!"

Jesus was pushed roughly down on his knees. But prisoners were in no position to complain about their captors' behaviour. One of the soldiers found a piece of purple cloth and draped it over Jesus's shoulders as if it were a princely cloak. It hid the cuts and bruises from the flogging that Pilate had ordered. Laughing, one guard twisted thorny branches into a crown and pushed it onto Jesus's head. Someone else thrust a reed into his trembling hands.

"Here is your sceptre, Your Majesty."

"Can we get you anything to make you more comfortable, Your Majesty?"

A Roman centurion strode into the room, looking at Jesus in his princely garb while the soldiers around him jumped to attention.

"We've got our orders, boys," barked the centurion. "Get that prisoner on his feet – we're going to Golgotha."

One of the soldiers replaced the purple cloak with Jesus's own worn robes. Others placed a wooden beam across the prisoner's shoulders. It was heavy and Jesus, already half-dead from the flogging the soldiers had given him, nearly collapsed under its weight.

The centurion pushed open the dungeon doors and sunlight flooded through. It was a strangely beautiful day for a crucifixion. As Jesus dragged the heavy beam through the winding city streets, people were waiting outside, not to greet Jesus as a messiah, but to watch the condemned man. The streets were packed, but there was no sign of the disciples anywhere. Only a few women still loyal to the Messiah were in the crowds, holding out jugs of water for the condemned man.

On the summit of Golgotha, a hill that looked very much like a skull, there were two other men, both thieves, who would also die today. Three enormous timbers had been sunk upright into the ground. Jesus was made to lie on the ground. His hands were nailed to either end of the crossbeam. With ropes, Jesus was hauled up one of the poles and the crossbeam tied into position. His feet were nailed in place and a sign declaring his crime pinned above his head:

JESUS OF NAZARETH.
KING OF THE JEWS

"Father," cried Jesus. "Forgive them, for they do not know what they do."

The priests, who were there to ensure no one came to save Jesus before he died, started taunting him.

"He raised many from death but, look, the Messiah is not able to save himself."

"Yes," cried others. "Jesus, you claimed that you could destroy the temple and rebuild it in three days – why don't you save yourself now?"

A soldier dipped a sponge in wine mixed with vinegar.

"Drink this, it will dull the pain."

Jesus shook his head. On either side of him were the thieves, struggling against the pain of the iron spikes in their hands and ankles.

"Hey," said one, turning his head towards Jesus with a sneer, "if you really are the Messiah, why can't you save yourself? And why can't you save us, while you're about it?"

"Be quiet," said the other thief. "Don't you fear God at all? We die today for our crimes, but Jesus has done nothing wrong! Why have they done this to you, teacher? Remember me when you return as King, Jesus."

"Even today," replied Jesus, "you shall be with me in paradise."

He struggled to look down at his mother, his friend Mary Magdalen and the other women who had followed him, and at John, the only disciple who had not fled into hiding.

"Take my mother home, John. Look after her while I am gone."

It was noon, the time of day when the sun should have been at its fiercest, but thick clouds were building up in the sky. Darkness settled over the land.

Jesus could hardly speak now. The pain from his hands and feet had spread all over his body. Cramp wracked his arms and legs. Thirst clawed at his throat and each breath seemed a gasp. The afternoon wore slowly on. First one, then the other of the two thieves stopped breathing. A centurion pierced their sides with the point of lance; it was his duty to make sure they were dead.

"Father," Jesus gasped through his pain, "why have you abandoned me?"

"He is calling the prophets," jeered the crowd.

The centurion offered Jesus more wine and vinegar. But Jesus did not hear the jeers of the crowd or the centurion's voice. The Messiah raised his face slowly, painfully, towards the darkened sky.

"Father, it is finished."

Then the last whisper of breath escaped his body and his head fell forward. Jesus was dead.

In Jerusalem, the curtain in the temple split in two. The ground shook and all over the country and rocks split in two. It was only three in the afternoon but the day was as dark as night.

The centurion reached up to lance Jesus's side.

"Truly," he said, "this man was the Son of God."

The Empty Tomb

...Mary stood weeping outside the tomb.
As she wept, she bent over to look into the tomb;
and she saw two angels in white, sitting where
the body of Jesus had been lying...

JOHN 20:11–12

It was not yet light when Mary Magdalene, one of Jesus's closest followers and friends, set out to visit his tomb on the first day of the week. She had precious spices to sprinkle on his body, but now that a great stone had been rolled across the entrance to the tomb, who would let her in?

The evening after the Messiah's death, Joseph of Arimathea, a wealthy and influential follower of Jesus, asked Pilate to give him the body. Pilate ordered it to be done, and Joseph took Jesus's body to his own new tomb, close to Golgotha. Joseph and another friend of Jesus, Nicodemus, had wrapped his body in strips of clean linen, sprinkling them with costly fragrances according to Jewish ritual. In this way, Jesus had been hurriedly buried the very same day he died, before the Sabbath, as was the custom.

As Mary reached the garden where the tomb was, she noticed that the stone at the entrance had been rolled aside. Was someone else adding spices to the linen or had the grave been attacked by robbers? Cautiously, she looked inside: the tomb was empty.

Mary hurried to Peter and John, who were in hiding in a house nearby.

"Peter… John… it's gone! Jesus's body has gone. Come and see."

The disciples ran through the streets barefoot. Surely not even the priests would dare desecrate a holy grave? Perhaps it was the work of grave robbers, hoping to steal jewellery.

John reached the tomb first. He looked in and saw it was exactly as Mary had described – linen strips lay on the floor, but Jesus's body had disappeared. Peter, coming up behind him, pointed to a piece of cloth left neatly on the stone where the body had lain. It had been used to cover Jesus's face. What kind of thief would stop to fold it?

"We must tell the others about this," said Peter. "Mary, come with us. It might not be safe to stay here."

But Mary decided to linger – with Jesus dead, there seemed to be no point in going home. She wanted to be here, where she had last seen the Master.

"Woman, why do you weep?"

Mary looked up from her jar of spices in surprise. A light was shining out of the tomb. Two men, both dressed in white, were sitting on the stone where Jesus had lain, one at the head, one at the feet.

"They have taken away the body of my Lord," she said, "and I do not know where they have hidden him."

"He is not here," said one of the men. "Why do you seek that which is gone?"

Perhaps these two are the thieves who have taken the body, she thought, even if they don't look like grave robbers or temple guards sent by the Sanhedrin. Maybe she should fetch Joseph of Arimathea – he would persuade

them, shame the men into revealing what they had done with Jesus's body. There would still be time to give him a second burial…

"Woman, why are you weeping? Whom do you seek?"

Another man was standing behind her, his face hidden in the shadows of an olive tree. Was he the gardener?

"They have taken the body of my master away!" she said, hot tears of frustration running down her cheeks.

"Sir, if you or your friends have taken him away, please tell me where I can find him."

The man stepped out of the shadows into the morning light.

"Mary."

She knew the voice at once. A chill went through her.

"Master!"

"Go to the disciples and tell them what you have seen, Mary. Tell them that I am on my way to my Father."

"Yes, Teacher."

Mary ran out of the garden, her jar of costly spices lying forgotten on the ground. She wanted to shout for joy, to dance along the street like a child. Everyone in the world should share in the good news.

"I have seen Jesus," she gasped, bursting into the house where the disciples were all gathered in hiding. "He is alive! He spoke to me. Jesus has come back to us. He is risen!"

On the Road to Emmaus

"Oh, how foolish you are, and how slow of heart . . .
Was it not necessary that the Messiah should suffer
these things and then enter into his glory?"

LUKE 24:25–26

The two men on the road to the village of Emmaus, some seven miles outside Jerusalem, had only one thing to talk about.

"Jesus is risen!"

"They say the teacher is alive!"

They had been followers of Jesus and they wished the rumours were true.

Deep in discussion about what this would mean, the two men did not take the time to look at the new traveller who joined them, his face wrapped in cloth against the dusty wind.

"What is this conversation you are holding as you walk?" he asked.

"Are you the only traveller from Jerusalem not to hear the news?" said the elder of the men, whose name was Cleopas. "We were followers of Jesus – a prophet we hoped would deliver the people of Israel, the true Messiah. Our chief priests condemned him to death and it's been three days since his burial, yet this morning, a woman we know claims that she has just seen him – alive!

Other women who knew Jesus amazed

us by saying that when they went to visit his body, the tomb was indeed empty. As the women stood at the entrance to the tomb, two angels appeared and told them that Jesus is risen from the dead! Some of us went to see for ourselves, but, though the tomb was indeed empty, we did not see the master."

"Was it not said by the prophets that the Messiah shall rise from the dead?" said the stranger. "Why do you have such little faith?"

They reached Emmaus and Cleopas invited the stranger to sup with them. Bowls of food were laid on the table, the wine poured.

The stranger removed his travelling cloak. His head now bare, he broke the bread with his hands and held it up.

"My Father, bless this food we are about to eat."

At that moment, the two men recognised their fellow traveller – it was Jesus. The Messiah.

"Lord, forgive us…"

Even as Cleopas spoke, Jesus was no longer there.

The two men were sure of what they had seen; they had felt Jesus all the time they walked together, but had been too absorbed in their talk to heed what their hearts sensed. They hurried out into the stormy night, back to Jerusalem – they had to tell others the news.

"Mary was right," they cried, hugging each other for joy. "Jesus is alive! This is not the end of his story. This is only the beginning."

Thomas the Doubter

But Thomas... said to them,
"Unless I see the mark of the nails in his hands,
and put my finger in the mark of the nails
and my hand in his side, I will not believe."

JOHN 20:24–25

The disciples were gathered behind locked doors, still afraid to go out in broad daylight in case they were picked up by the temple guards.

"I tell you we saw him! Jesus was here in our midst."

"If only you were here to meet him too, Thomas. It is a shame you were out buying food at the time."

Thomas, one of the disciples, looked doubtful.

"Apparently almost everyone but me has seen our master: Mary says she spoke to him; Cleopas and his friend claim they met him on the road to Emmaus; even Peter will have me believe Jesus visited you here."

"But he was here, Thomas," insisted one of the others. "He appeared out of nowhere while we were talking and he said, 'Peace be with you.'"

"Grief does strange things to people," replied Thomas. "It can make them start seeing things."

"This was no ghost," said Mark. "Jesus ate fish right in front of us. Has a spirit flesh, has it bones?"

Thomas shook his head.

"If I can't see the print of the nails in his hands and touch them, or place my finger in the lance wound in his side, I will not believe that it is really Jesus come back to us."

"You would feel differently if you had

been here, Thomas," said one of other men. "We are certain it was Jesus who came to us."

As he spoke, the lamps flickered at one end of the room and a man stood there, his head framed by the light.

"Peace be with you."

The man reached out to Thomas.

"Thomas, give me your hand."

Thomas held out a trembling hand and let the man guide it.

"Put your fingers here and here. Do you feel the print of the nails on my hands? Place your hand on my side – can you feel the wound made by the centurion's lance? Stop doubting me, Thomas. Believe."

It really was Jesus standing in front him – truly the master had come back from the dead. He was risen! How could Thomas have doubted all this time? Instantly he was filled with shame, but also with joy. So much joy that he could hardly breathe.

"My Lord," he whispered, "my God."

"Thomas, you have believed because you have seen me," said Jesus, raising his voice so that all the disciples could hear his words. "But I say to you: Blessed are those who do not see… and yet believe."

And a moment later he was gone.

Breakfast by the Lake

Just after daybreak, Jesus stood on the beach;
but the disciples did not know it was Jesus...
When they had gone ashore, they saw a charcoal
fire there, with fish on it, and bread.

JOHN 21:4, 9

Peter and some other disciples had been fishing all night. The disciples had all returned to Galilee so there were lots of mouths to feed.

A man called to them from the shore, "Have you caught much?"

"Not a single fish," admitted James.

"Cast your net on the right side of the boat," said the man, "and you will catch some."

The disciples did as the man asked and, within minutes, their nets were full

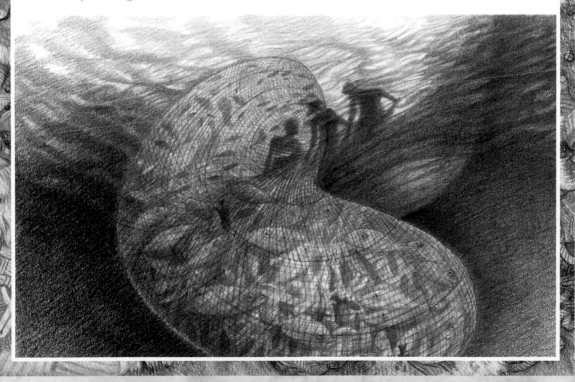

to breaking with countless fish, jumping and shimmering in the sunlight.

"It is Jesus who called to us," said John. "This is yet another of his miracles."

Peter looked up sharply from his basket. Was it really Jesus with them again? In Galilee?

Ever since the night Jesus died, Peter had been troubled about his denial of the Lord. Not once, not twice, but three times he had let the master down and every time he saw him, his heart was flooded with shame.

"I am sure it is the master himself standing on the shore, too," added John. Now that dawn was breaking, they could see the man better.

Peter grabbed his robe and put it on. He was not sure he was ready to speak to Jesus yet. Behind his locked door, in his darkened room, it had seemed easy for Peter to hide his guilt away. And when all the disciples were together, Peter could conceal himself at the back of the group and avoid Jesus's gaze. But now it was just a few of them. In the harsh dawn light, Jesus would definitely see him. What if the master revealed Peter's shame to the others? How could he, one of the chosen twelve, live with such humiliation?

James and John moored the boat. Jesus had lit a fire and was cooking fish on it. He had bread, too, in a small wicker basket at his side.

"Bring some of your fish," he called out. "Come, have some breakfast."

John put more fish on the hot charcoal. The others huddled close to the fire, thankful for its warmth – the dawn was cold. Jesus held out some bread and Peter took it, though he struggled to swallow each mouthful. Thomas turned the spit over the fire and the others began to wolf down the bread and fish – food tasted good after you'd been working hard all night – but Peter sat paralysed.

"Peter, son of John," he said, "do you love me more than these?"

For a moment Peter's throat tightened and he could not speak. Was Jesus going to reproach him? Was he going to send Peter away?

"You know that I love you, Lord," he mumbled hurriedly.

"Then feed my lambs," said Jesus.

Peter could not tear his eyes away from Jesus's steady gaze.

"Peter, son of John," asked Jesus again, "do you love me?"

"You know I do," replied Peter.

Why had Jesus asked him the same question twice? Was he going to reveal Peter's betrayal to the others?

"Then tend my sheep, Peter" he said.

What could Jesus mean? Peter felt the eyes of the other disciples on him.

"Peter," asked Jesus for a third time. "Do you love me?"

"But you know that I do," cried Peter. "You know everything, Lord. You know I love you."

There, he had said it three times now – once for every time he had denied the master on that terrible night.

"Then feed my sheep," repeated Jesus.

Suddenly Peter knew exactly what those strange words meant. Jesus called himself the good shepherd and his flock were the people who accepted his word and who then lived according to his teachings.

Peter realised that the Lord was telling him that he still wanted Peter to be a disciple, to carry on the work Jesus had begun, helping people to discover the Lord's teachings and follow him!

Jesus not just forgiven him, he had given Peter a job to do.

The Ascension

"Go therefore and make disciples of all nations, baptizing them in the name of the Father and of the Son and of the Holy Spirit... And remember, I am with you always, to the end of the age."

MATTHEW 28:19–20

It had been six weeks since Jesus had risen from the dead, six weeks in which the disciples had all seen him with their own eyes, touched him with their own hands and spoken with him. No doubt remained in their minds that the Messiah had conquered death itself and now walked among the living!

"My work with you is done," said Jesus as they stood on the Mount of Olives outside Jerusalem. "It was written in the scriptures that the Christ should suffer and on the third day rise from the dead, and so it has happened. It is time for me to return to my Father in heaven. But I shall always be with you."

The disciples were silent. None could believe Jesus was leaving them forever.

"My friends," said Jesus, looking into their sad eyes. "All authority over heaven and earth has been given to me. You will heal the sick and speak in new languages so that others will know you are my disciples. God will send you his Holy Spirit. He will fill you with courage, that you may spread the good news all over Jerusalem, in Judea, in Samaria and throughout the whole world – those who believe in me and are baptised will be saved!"

The sun broke over the horizon and a strong breeze blew across the hill. The disciples all saw Jesus rising into heaven. They moved forward as one, reaching out.

"Master," called out Peter.

But a cloud moved across the reddening sky, hiding Jesus from view.

"People of Galilee, why do you stare into heaven?"

Glancing away from the cloud that had hidden Jesus, the disciples saw two men standing under the olive trees, both robed in dazzling white.

"Do not weep," said one of them. "This Jesus who was taken from you up into heaven will return."

He will return! The disciples knew what the men, the angels, had said was true. Jesus would come back one day, when the time was right, as he had promised. He would return to welcome everyone who believed in him into heaven itself.

Praising God and his Son, the disciples set off back to Jerusalem.

The Day of Pentecost

And suddenly from heaven there came a sound like the rush of a violent wind... Divided tongues, as of fire, appeared among them... All of them were filled with the Holy Spirit and began to speak in other languages, as the Spirit gave them ability.

ACTS 2:2–4

"You will heal the sick and speak in new languages," Jesus had said to the disciples, before he returned to heaven to be with his Father. The men, dumbfounded at their master being taken away from them, had hardly given those words another thought or considered what he could have meant. Until the feast day, the day of the harvest festival when people from all over the country came to the temple in Jerusalem with the first precious fruit and grain from their harvest.

On that holy feast day, the disciples were gathered in a house somewhere in the great city. Mary, Jesus's mother, was with them. As they sat talking, Peter became aware of a strange noise nearby.

"Can you hear that, brothers?"

"Yes, we can."

The noise grew – it sounded as if a great wind were rushing through the windows, yet nothing in the room stirred, nothing moved.

Suddenly tongues of flame appeared above every person's head.

"It is a message from Jesus," said John, but he didn't speak in his own language. He spoke in a language he had never known before. The other disciples were not frightened by this, for they were all filled with the Holy Spirit and they all started talking at once, each in a different language, one that they had never learned or spoken.

"Jesus's promise has come true," cried Matthew. "We are speaking in tongues. The Holy Spirit has come!"

The sound of the wind had attracted the people walking past on the city streets and now they came rushing to see what had happened. The disciples had to push through the crowds to get out of the house.

"What is the matter, friend?"

"Nothing at all," said Peter, speaking in a strange language.

"They have drunk too much wine," said one man.

"Wine might loosen your tongue," said another, "but it does not make you talk like a learned scribe. I am from Egypt and yet I can understand every single word this man says."

"Men of Judea and all who dwell in Jerusalem," shouted Peter at the passers-by. "Listen to my words! Let this be known to you: Jesus of Nazareth was killed as promised in the Scriptures, but God raised him up, for death had no hold over him."

Many who heard Peter speak were touched by his words, by his enthusiasm and conviction.

"Tell us what to do," they said.

"Repent and be baptised – every one of you – in the name of Jesus Christ and your sins will be forgiven," replied Peter. "Then you shall receive the gift of the Holy Spirit. For the promise is to you and your children and all those who come after you."

Word of the miracle soon spread around Jerusalem. Visitors from Libya and Egypt, from the kingdoms of Persia and Babylonia, people who lived in Jerusalem but came originally from far away lands like the island of Crete or the mighty city of Rome, all came to hear the disciples, these poor, uneducated Galileans, who talked fluently in their own languages.

The disciples scattered on to the streets of Jerusalem, talking fervently about Jesus, spreading his word, telling people the good news about the Son of God who died for everyone's sins. They were filled with courage and passion. There was no place for fear in their hearts, no space anymore for doubt in their minds. Jesus was still with them after all. He was still leading them.

Three thousand people accepted Jesus into their hearts that day. Three thousand were baptised and changed their lives, devoting their time to the disciples' teaching, selling all they had and giving the money to the needy. The new believers met to break bread together in the name of the Lord, and their hearts were filled with joy. In time, many more would follow them. They would spread the word of Jesus to every corner of the world, till the earth itself echoed with the joy of his salvation.

The Bible Lands

The stories retold in this book are about actual events. They
happened to real people in real places, many, many years ago.
The two maps that follow show some of the different places
we have visited in CHILDREN'S STORIES FROM THE BIBLE.

The first map shows the whole of the Bible Lands,
from Mount Ararat, where Noah's ark came to rest,
to Mount Sinai, where Moses received God's laws.
The second map focuses in on the Holy Lands, from
Mount Hermon down to the Dead Sea in the south.
Discover where Jesus was born, where he lived
and the places where he taught and spoke.

BLACK SEA

ASIA MINOR
(TURKEY)

MT ARARAT

ASSYRIA

Nineveh •

PERSIA

Tarsus
•

Haran
•

CYPRUS

ARAM

Susa
•

MEDITERRANEAN
SEA

Sidon
•

CANAAN
(ISRAEL) →

SEA OF
GALILEE

Babylon
•

BABYLONIA

Jericho •
Jerusalem •

MOAB

Ur
•

DEAD SEA

GOSHEN

SINAI ←

MT SINAI/HOREB ←

River Nile

RED SEA

MAP OF THE
BIBLE LANDS

0   1 INCH   150 miles
0   25MM   240 km

CUSH
(ETHIOPIA)

▲ Mountain   • Town or city

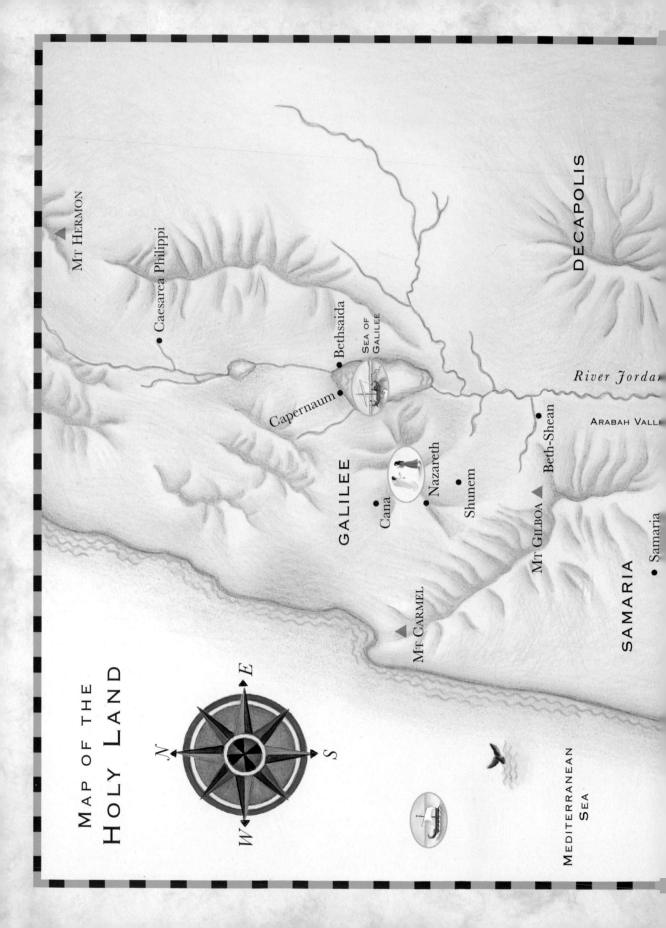

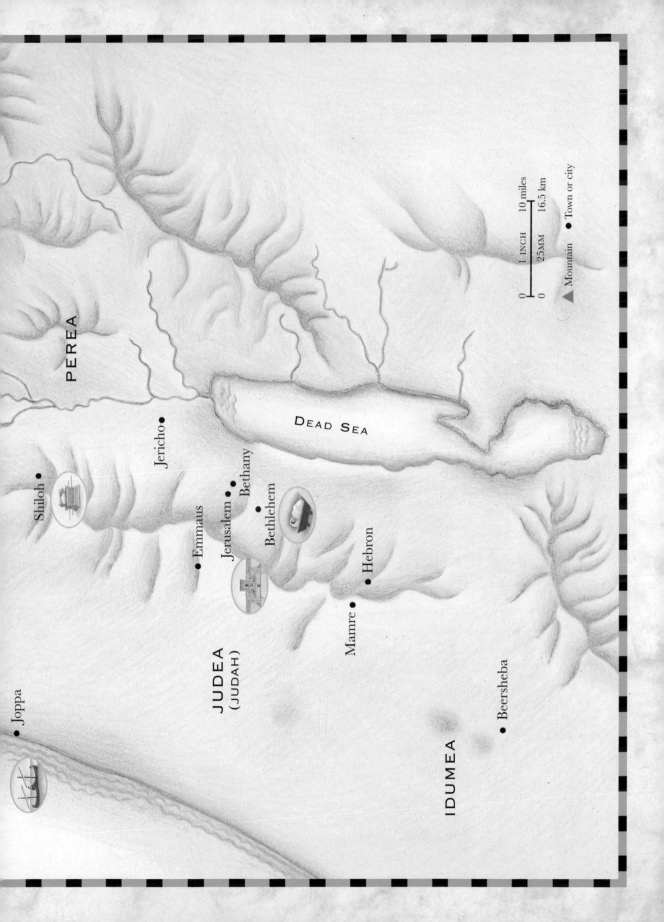

PEREA

DEAD SEA

Joppa

Shiloh

Jericho

Emmaus

Jerusalem
Bethany

Bethlehem

JUDEA
(JUDAH)

Mamre

Hebron

IDUMEA

Beersheba

0   1 INCH   10 miles

0   25MM   16.5 km

▲ Mountain   ● Town or city

Timeline of the Old Testament

These are some of the key dates relating to the people and events in the Old Testament.

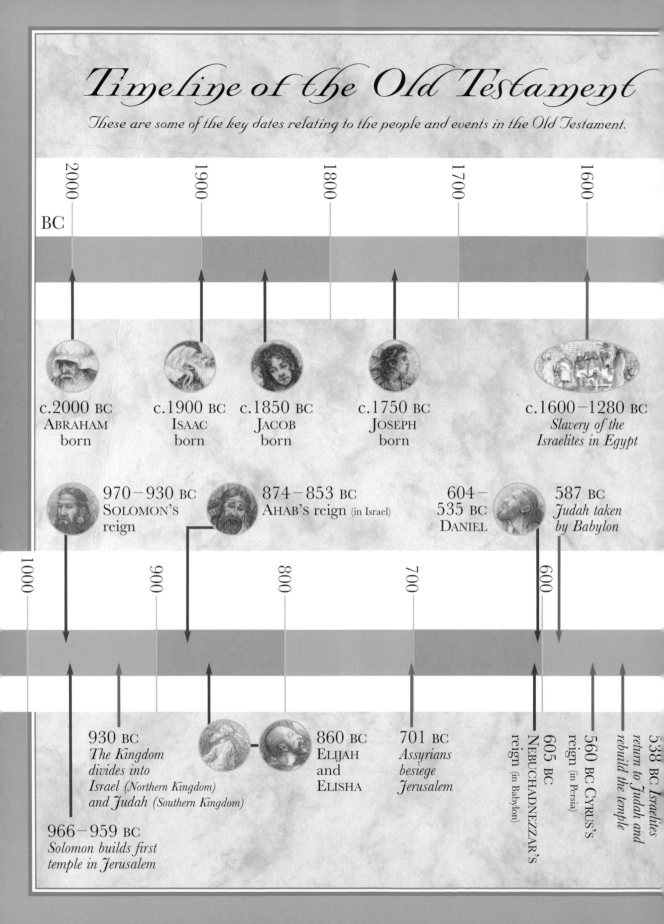

2000

1900

1800

1700

1600

BC

c.2000 BC
ABRAHAM
born

c.1900 BC
ISAAC
born

c.1850 BC
JACOB
born

c.1750 BC
JOSEPH
born

c.1600–1280 BC
Slavery of the
Israelites in Egypt

970–930 BC
SOLOMON'S
reign

874–853 BC
AHAB'S reign (in Israel)

604–
535 BC
DANIEL

587 BC
Judah taken
by Babylon

1000

900

800

700

600

930 BC
The Kingdom
divides into
Israel (Northern Kingdom)
and Judah (Southern Kingdom)

860 BC
ELIJAH
and
ELISHA

701 BC
Assyrians
besiege
Jerusalem

NEBUCHADNEZZAR'S
reign (in Babylon)

605 BC

560 BC CYRUS'S
reign (in Persia)

538 BC Israelites
return to Judah and
rebuild the temple

966–959 BC
Solomon builds first
temple in Jerusalem

c.1115 BC
ELI

1050–
1010 BC
SAUL'S reign

c.1270 BC
JOSHUA
born

c.1230 BC
*Entry of
Israelites
into Canaan*

1400

1300

1200

1100

1000

c.1350 BC
MOSES
born

1280 BC
*Exodus
from Egypt*

c.1100 BC
RUTH

c.1075 BC
SAMUEL

1010–
970 BC
DAVID'S
reign

400

300

200

100

0

BC AD

50 BC
*Walls of
Jerusalem rebuilt*

63 BC
*Romans
occupy
Jerusalem*

*The 'c.' before some dates means circa (around).
We use this when the exact date of an event is not known.*

Timeline of the New Testament

These are some of the key dates relating to the people and events in the New Testament.

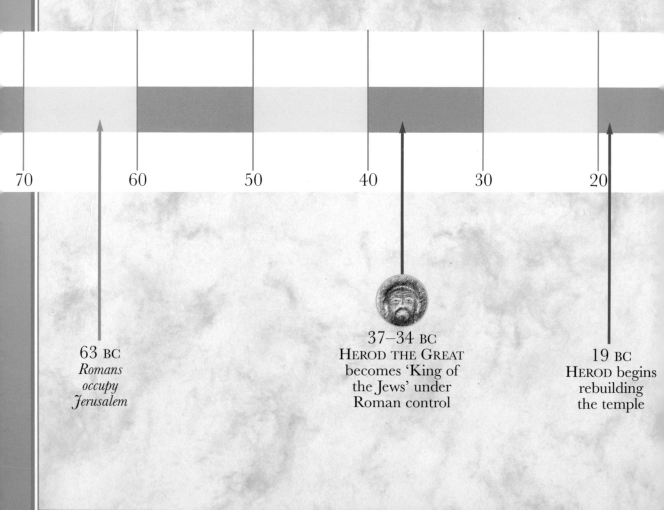

| 70 | 60 | 50 | 40 | 30 | 20 |

63 BC
Romans occupy Jerusalem

37–34 BC
HEROD THE GREAT becomes 'King of the Jews' under Roman control

19 BC
HEROD begins rebuilding the temple

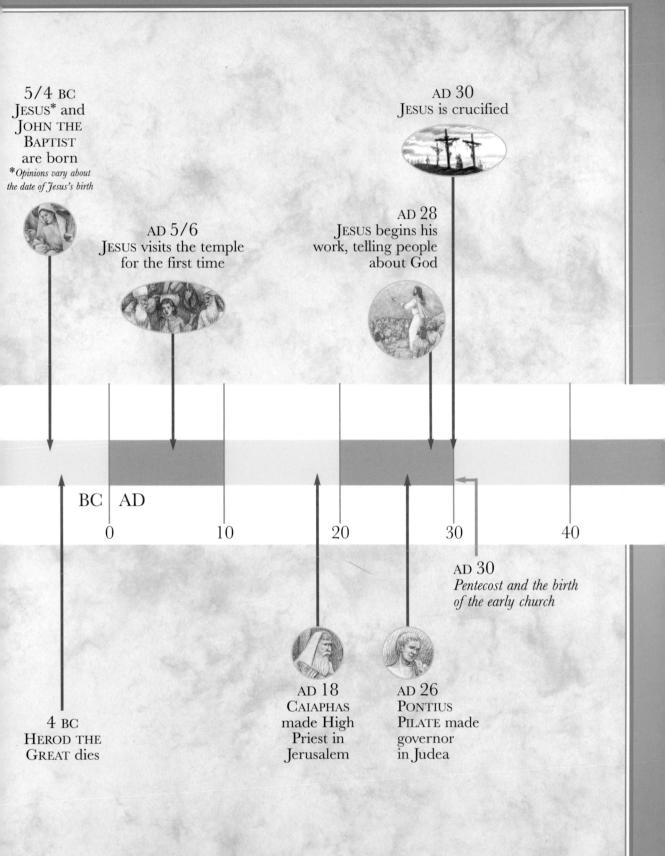

5/4 BC
JESUS* and
JOHN THE
BAPTIST
are born
*Opinions vary about
the date of Jesus's birth

AD 30
JESUS is crucified

AD 5/6
JESUS visits the temple
for the first time

AD 28
JESUS begins his
work, telling people
about God

BC AD

0   10   20   30   40

AD 30
*Pentecost and the birth
of the early church*

4 BC
HEROD THE
GREAT dies

AD 18
CAIAPHAS
made High
Priest in
Jerusalem

AD 26
PONTIUS
PILATE made
governor
in Judea

People in the Bible

These are some of the key people you will find in

CHILDREN'S STORIES FROM THE BIBLE

AARON
Moses's elder brother and helper, and the first anointed high priest.

ABEL
Adam and Eve's second child, murdered by his jealous brother Cain.

ABRAHAM
God changed Abram's name to Abraham (father of nations) and promised to make him the founder of the Hebrew nation. When he and his wife, Sarah, were both old, God gave them a son, Isaac, who was both to test Abraham's faithful trust in God and to be the first in the promised nation.

ADAM
The first man, created by God and put in charge of the Garden of Eden.

AHAB
A king of Israel who married Jezebel and was condemned by the prophet Elijah for his worship of the pagan god Baal.

ANDREW
A fisherman from Capernaum, Peter's brother and one of Jesus's first disciples.

ANNAS
A Jewish high priest and father-in-law of Caiaphas.

ASHER
One of Jacob's twelve sons.

BALTHASAR
No one with this name appears in the Bible text but traditionally it has become linked with one of the wise men (or astrologers) who visited the infant Jesus in Bethlehem. Similarly, his companions have become known by the names of Caspar and Melchior.

BARABBAS
A murderer and rebel freed by Pontius Pilate. The crowd voted to free him and put Jesus of Nazareth to death instead.

BARTHOLOMEW
One of Jesus's twelve disciples. Some believe that he and Nathanael are one and the same person.

BELSHAZZAR
A Babylonian ruler who was warned of his downfall by Daniel.

BENJAMIN
Jacob's youngest son and Joseph's brother. (Their mother was Rachel.)

BEZALEL
A skilled crafts person in charge of making the tabernacle when the Israelites were wandering in the desert.

BOAZ
A wealthy farmer and land-owner from Bethlehem who married the widow, Ruth

and became the great-grandfather of King David.

CAIAPHAS
The high priest in Jerusalem when Jesus was working with his disciples, and before whom Jesus stood trial.

CAIN
The elder son of Adam and Eve, who killed his brother Abel out of jealousy.

CAESAR
The title 'Caesar' was given to Roman emperors in New Testament times. Augustus ruled at the time when Jesus was born and Tiberius was his successor.

CALEB
One of twelve spies Moses sent to find out about Canaan, the Promised Land, and its people.

CASPAR
See Balthasar.

CLEOPAS
One of the two followers of Jesus who met him on the day of his resurrection, walking along the road to Emmaus.

DAN
One of Jacob's twelve sons.

DANIEL
An exiled Jew who rose to prominence in the Babylonian Court and served several kings. He interpreted the dreams of King Nebuchadnezzar and showed his faith in God when he was thrown to the lions.

DAVID
Israel's second and greatest king, and an ancestor of Jesus. He was a shepherd boy when he killed the Philistine giant Goliath. Samuel anointed him king in place of Saul.

DELILAH
The Philistine woman who charmed Samson to discover the secret of his strength and then betrayed him to her people.

ELI
A priest at Shiloh and the guardian of the boy, Samuel.

ELIEZER
Abraham's chief servant who, it is thought, was entrusted to choose a wife for Isaac.

ELIJAH
A prophet of Israel, famous for his victory over the prophets of Baal on Mount Carmel. When his work was finished a chariot of fire took him to heaven.

ELIMELECH
The husband of Naomi.

ELISHA
Elijah's successor, a leading prophet of Israel and a well known miracle-worker.

ELIZABETH
The wife of Zechariah and mother of John, later known as 'John the Baptist'. Elizabeth was a relation of Mary, the mother of Jesus.

ELKANAH
The husband of Hannah and father of Samuel.

ESAU
Isaac's son and (elder) twin brother of Jacob. He sold his birthright to Jacob in exchange for a bowl of stew.

ESTHER
A Jewish queen of Persia. She risked her life to foil a plot to destroy the Jews. This is commemorated in the annual Jewish festival of Purim.

EVE
The first woman created by God, Eve lived in the Garden of Eden until she was tempted to disobey God.

GABRIEL
An angel, one of God's messengers. Gabriel is one of only three angels to be named in the canonical Bible.

GAD
One of Jacob's twelve sons.

GEHAZI
The prophet Elisha's servant.

GOLIATH
The giant Philistine champion, who was defeated by a single blow in the famous fight with the shepherd boy, David. David became king of Israel.

HAM
One of Noah's sons.

HAMAN
The enemy of Mordecai, his plot against the Jews was foiled by Queen Esther.

HANNAH
The mother of Samuel who was born in answer to her prayers for a son. She later gave her son over to God's service and he grew up to become a prophet.

HEROD, KING
Herod the Great, the ruler of Judea under Roman occupation, around the time of the birth of Jesus of Nazareth.

HEROD ANTIPAS
Son of Herod the Great, Herod Antipas ordered the execution of John the Baptist.

HEROD PHILIP
A brother of Herod Antipas.

HERODIAS
The wife of Herod Antipas, who made her daughter ask for the head of John the Baptist.

ISAAC
Abraham and Sarah's son, God used him to test his father's faith. Later, he married Rebekah and they had twin sons, Esau and Jacob.

ISRAEL
The name given to Jacob after he encountered the angel. His descendants were the Israelites.

ISSACHAR
One of Jacob's twelve sons.

JACOB
One of Isaac and Rebekah's twin sons (the brother of Esau). He was the ancestor of the twelve tribes of Israel.

JAIRUS
A leader of the synagogue in Capernaum who asked Jesus to heal his daughter.

JAMES
The son of Alphaeus. One of Jesus's twelve disciples, about whom very little is known.

JAMES
Son of Zebedee. The brother of the disciple John, he left his work as a fisherman on Lake Galilee to become one of the twelve disciples, the closest friends of Jesus.

JAPHETH
One of Noah's sons.

JESSE
The grandson of Boaz and Ruth, and father of King David.

JESUS OF NAZARETH
Throughout the Old Testament there were many prophecies about God's promised Messiah (God's chosen deliverer) and Christians believe these were fulfilled in the birth, life, death, resurrection and ascension of

Jesus. These are described in the four Gospels and Book of Acts in the New Testament of the Bible. Christians believe Jesus to be the Son of God, the Lord and Saviour of the world, and also call him Jesus Christ ('Christ' was a Greek word, meaning 'Messiah'). The name Jesus means 'saviour'.

JETHRO
A Midianite priest and father-in-law of Moses.

JEZEBEL
The wife of King Ahab and a devout follower of Baal.

JOHN
(THE DISCIPLE)
The son of Zebedee and brother of the disciple James. He was one of Jesus's closest disciples and wrote a number of New Testament books: the gospel that bears his name, the three letters and also, possibly, the book of Revelation.

JOHN THE BAPTIST
Son of Zechariah and Elizabeth and a relative of Jesus, he lived in the wilderness as an adult. He prepared the way for Jesus, preaching a message of repentance and baptizing many people (including Jesus) in the River Jordan. He was executed by Herod Antipas.

JONAH
A prophet of God. Little is known about him other than the remarkable story of

his reluctance to take God's message to Nineveh.

JONATHAN
Saul's eldest son and a close and loyal friend of David. He was killed, with his father, by the Philistines.

JOSEPH, HUSBAND OF MARY
A descendant of David and husband of Jesus's mother, Mary. He was a carpenter in the hilltop village of Nazareth.

JOSEPH
Jacob's favourite son, who was sold into slavery by his jealous brothers. He used his God-given ability to interpret dreams and became an official appointed by the pharaoh and was finally happily reunited with his family.

JOSEPH OF ARIMATHEA
A member of the Jewish council who arranged for Jesus's body to be buried in the tomb he had prepared for himself.

JOSHUA
One of the twelve spies sent to explore Canaan, the Promised Land. He became Moses's successor and led the people of Israel across the River Jordan, into Canaan. Joshua is best known for leading the Israelites during the battle of Jericho.

JUDAH
One of Jacob's twelve sons. The southern kingdom was named after him.

JUDAS ISCARIOT
One of Jesus's twelve disciples, with responsibility for their money. He betrayed Jesus for 30 silver pieces. He later regretted his action and took his own life.

LABAN
The uncle of Jacob and father of his wives Leah and Rachel.

LAZARUS
Brother of Mary and Martha, and a friend of Jesus, who raised him from the dead.

LEAH
Laban's oldest daughter whom he tricked Jacob into marrying.

LEVI
One of Jacob's twelve sons.

LUKE
A doctor and the Gentile author of the Bible books of the gospel of Luke and the Acts of the Apostles.

MARTHA
The hard-working sister of Lazarus and Mary. Jesus often stayed with the family.

MARY, MOTHER OF JESUS
The wife of Joseph of Nazareth and the earthly mother of Jesus.

MARY
The sister of Lazarus and Martha, Mary was an eager follower of Jesus.

MARY MAGDALENE
A follower of Jesus and the first person to see him after the resurrection.

MATTHEW
Also called Levi, he was a former tax-collector before becoming one of Jesus's twelve disciples. He is reputed to be the author of Matthew's Gospel in the Bible.

MELCHIOR
See Balthasar.

MICHAL
King Saul's younger daughter and one of David's wives.

MIRIAM
Moses and Aaron's sister, who was with them in the desert.

MORDECAI
Esther's cousin and guardian.

MOSES
The great leader who freed the Israelites from slavery in Egypt and led them to the borders of Canaan. He is famous for many events, notably for receiving from God the Ten Commandments and instructions for building the tabernacle on Mount Sinai.

NAOMI
The mother-in-law of Ruth.

NAPHTALI
One of Jacob's twelve sons.

NATHANAEL
See Bartholomew.

NEBUCHADNEZZAR
The king of Babylon at the time of the exile of the Israelites.

NOAH
A good man who obeyed God by building an ark to save his family and two of every kind of creature from the flood.

OBED
Boaz and Ruth's son and grandfather of King David.

ORPAH
One of Naomi's two Moabite daughters-in-law.

PETER
A fisherman, he was one of Jesus's closest disciples. Originally named Simon, Jesus renamed him Peter, meaning 'rock' – a reference to the position he would come to hold in the church. With Jesus during all the crucial events of his ministry, Peter proclaimed him the Messiah on the day of Pentecost. Two books of the New Testament bear his name.

PHARAOH
The title of the kings of Egypt. Several pharaohs are mentioned in the Old Testament, including the pharaoh who made Joseph his chief minister and the pharaoh who was forced to let Moses lead the Israelites out of Egypt.

PHILIP
One of the twelve disciples, he came from Bethsaida.

PONTIUS PILATE
The Roman governor in Judea in AD 26–37. He presided over part of Jesus's trial and, to keep the peace, condemned Jesus to death.

POTIPHAR
An Egyptian official who bought Joseph as a slave.

RACHEL
Laban's beautiful, younger daughter and the favourite wife of Jacob. She was the mother of Joseph and Benjamin.

RAHAB
A brave woman from Jericho who gave protection to two of Joshua's spies.

REBEKAH
Isaac's wife and the mother of Esau and Jacob. She helped Jacob (her favourite son) trick his father into giving him the blessing due to Esau.

REHOBOAM
Solomon's son and leader of the southern kingdom of Judah when Israel was divided.

REUBEN
The eldest of Jacob's sons. He tried to save Joseph's life when his other brothers plotted to kill him out of jealousy.

RUTH
A young Moabite woman known for her loyalty to her Jewish mother-in-law, Naomi. She married Boaz and their son, Obed, was the grandfather of David.

SALOME
The daughter of Herodias whose famous dance led to the death of John the Baptist at Herod's command. Her name does not actually appear in the Bible texts.

SAMSON
An Israelite famed for his great physical strength. This ability was linked to a vow to God not to cut his hair. He was betrayed by Delilah and died while bringing down the Philistine temple.

SAMUEL
Dedicated to God's service from birth, he was a prophet who anointed Israel's first two kings, Saul and David.

SARAH
The wife of Abraham. In old age she became the mother of Isaac, fulfilling God's promise to Abraham.

SAUL
The first king of Israel. At first, he was a good king but later he deliberately disobeyed God and began to suffer fits of madness. He was killed, with his son, in a battle against the Philistines.

SHEM
The eldest son of Noah.

SIMEON
One of Jacob's twelve sons.

SIMON PETER
One of Jesus's twelve disciples. *See* Peter.

SIMON
One of Jesus's twelve disciples, also known as Simon the Zealot.

SOLOMON
The third king of Israel and son of David and Bathsheba. He is famous for his wisdom and the construction of the first temple in Jerusalem.

THADDEUS
One of Jesus's twelve disciples.

THOMAS
One of Jesus's disciples, who is best known for his doubts. He was absent when the others first saw the risen Jesus and refused to believe in the resurrection until he had seen and touched the wounds of Jesus for himself.

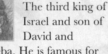

ZACCHAEUS
A tax collector in Jericho, Zacchaeus climbed into a tree so that he could see Jesus over the crowds. Jesus visited his house and after their encounter, Zacchaeus was a changed man.

ZEBULAN
One of Jacob's twelve sons.

ZECHARIAH
A priest, the husband of Elizabeth and the father of John the Baptist.

ZIPPORAH
The daughter of Jethro and the wife of Moses.

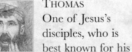

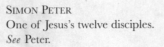

Glossary of Bible Words

ANGEL
A messenger from God. In the Bible, angels are sometimes winged creatures or they may resemble human beings.

ARK OF THE COVENANT
A wooden box covered in gold containing the stone tablets bearing God's Laws or Commandments, given to Moses.

BAPTISM
A ceremony of being washed in water as a sign of making a new beginning with God.

CHRIST
A Greek word meaning 'the anointed one' – chosen to be king.

CHRISTIAN
A person who follows Jesus and believes that he is the Christ.

COVENANT
A binding agreement, especially between God and people.

DISCIPLE
A student or learner. Jesus's special followers were named disciples.

FAITH
Belief and trust in something that cannot be scientifically proved.

GENTILE
A non-Jewish person.

GOD'S LAW
Instruction for right living. God's laws in the Bible were given to Moses on Mount Sinai (also known as Mount Horeb).

GOSPEL
An account of the life of Jesus.

ISRAEL
The name given to Jacob and his descendants; the nation – the people of Israel.

JEW
A descendant of the first people of Israel.

KINGDOM OF HEAVEN
Anywhere God is recognised as being in charge.

MESSIAH
The Hebrew word with the same meaning as 'Christ'.

MIRACLE
A special event that cannot easily be explained. Jews and Christians see miracles as signs that God is active in the world.

PARABLE
A story drawn from everyday life that is told to illustrate a spiritual truth.

PASSOVER
A meal the people of Israel ate just before Moses led them on the Exodus from slavery in Egypt. This Jewish festival is still celebrated each year.

PHARISEE
A strict Jewish religious group in the time of Jesus.

PROPHET
Someone who listens to God and delivers his message.

RABBI
A Jewish teacher of God's law in the synagogue.

RESURRECTION
Jesus's coming to life again after his death on the cross.

SABBATH
The one day in seven set aside in God's laws as a day of rest.

SACRIFICE
An offering made as an act of worship.

SADDUCEES
A religious group in the time of Jesus.

SANHEDRIN
The Jewish religious council in the time of Jesus.

SIN
Doing wrong; offending or turning away from God.

SON OF MAN
A phrase used by Jesus to describe himself as someone who, fully human, would have to die, but who would also usher in the Kingdom of God.

SYNAGOGUE
A Jewish place of worship, study and meeting.

TABERNACLE
A portable holy place used by the Israelites to worship God while they were wandering in the wilderness. Also used to house the ark of the covenant.

TEMPLE
A building where people worship God or gods. Solomon built the first temple to God in Jerusalem. Two further temples replaced this; the last temple (built by Herod the Great) was destroyed by the Romans in AD 70.

WORSHIP
Giving praise and honour to a god, person or thing you value greatly.

Favourite Bible Verses

❧ I will both lie down and sleep in peace;
for you alone, O Lord, make me lie down in safety.

PSALM 4:8

❧ The Lord is my shepherd, I shall not want.
He makes me lie down in green pastures;
he leads me beside still waters;
he restores my soul.
He leads me in right paths for his name's sake.

Even though I walk through the darkest valley, I fear no evil;
for you are with me; your rod and your staff – they comfort me.

You prepare a table before me in the presence of my enemies;
you anoint my head with oil; my cup overflows.
Surely goodness and mercy shall follow me all the days of my life,
and I shall dwell in the house of the Lord
my whole life long.

PSALM 23

The Lord is my light and my salvation; whom shall I fear?
The Lord is the stronghold of my life; of whom shall I be afraid?

PSALM 27:1

Praise the Lord, all you nations!
Extol him, all you peoples!
For great is his steadfast love towards us,
and the faithfulness of the Lord endures for ever.
Praise the Lord!

PSALM 117

For the Lord gives wisdom;
from his mouth come knowledge and understanding;
he stores up sound wisdom for the upright;
he is a shield to those who walk blamelessly,
guarding the paths of justice
and preserving the way of his faithful ones.

PROVERBS 2:6–8

The steadfast love of the Lord never ceases,
his mercies never come to an end;
they are new every morning;
great is your faithfulness.
"The Lord is my portion," says my soul.
"therefore I will hope in him."

LAMENTATIONS 3:22–24

"You have heard that it was said,
'You shall love your neighbour and hate your enemy.'
But I say to you, love your enemies and pray for those who persecute you,
so that you may be children of your Father in heaven;
for he makes his sun rise on the evil and on the good,
and sends rain on the righteous and the unrighteous."

MATTHEW 5:43–45

"Blessed are the poor in spirit, for theirs is the kingdom of heaven.
"Blessed are those who mourn, for they will be comforted.
"Blessed are the meek, for they will inherit the earth.
"Blessed are those who hunger and thirst for righteousness,
for they will be filled.
"Blessed are the merciful, for they will receive mercy.
"Blessed are the pure in heart, for they will see God.
"Blessed are the peacemakers, for they will be called the children of God.
"Blessed are those who are persecuted for righteousness' sake,
for theirs is the kingdom of heaven."

MATTHEW 5:1–10

"I give you a new commandment,
that you love one another.
Just as I have loved you,
you should also love one another.
By this everyone will know
that you are my disciples,
if you have love for one another."

JOHN 13:34–35

For God so loved the world that he gave his only Son,
so that everyone who believes in him may not perish
but may have eternal life.

JOHN 3:16

Beloved, let us love one another,
because love is from God;
everyone who loves is born of God and knows God.
Whoever does not love, does not know God, for God is love.
God's love was revealed to us in this way:
God sent his only Son into the world
so that we might live through him.

1 JOHN 4:7–10

Our Father in heaven, hallowed be your name.
Your kingdom come. Your will be done,
on earth as it is in heaven.
Give us this day our daily bread.
And forgive us our debts,
as we also have forgiven our debtors.
And do not bring us to the time of trial,
but rescue us from the evil one...

...For if you forgive others their trespasses,
your heavenly Father will also forgive you.

MATTHEW 6:9–14